T0115388

BETTER THAN RIGHT:
Appreciation, Beauty, Community

ELAINE EACHUS

authorHOUSE®

AuthorHouse™
1663 Liberty Drive
Bloomington, IN 47403
www.authorhouse.com
Phone: 833-262-8899

Published by AuthorHouse 04/30/2021

ISBN: 978-1-6655-2412-4 (sc)
ISBN: 978-1-6655-2420-9 (e)

Library of Congress Control Number: 2021908486

Print information available on the last page.

Cover Artwork by Jackson Eachus

This book is printed on acid-free paper.

CONTENTS

DEDICATION

Appreciation

I want to express my appreciation to those who have touched my life. We are part of a grand design that includes each of us in a tapestry, a world of many colors. Thank you for those who have supported and loved me, those who have challenged me and made me try to imagine your world. Thank you to my forebears who gave their legacy and to those who will yet leave their gifts on the altar of the world that God created. You have shaped me and tried to show me your world. Thank you.

This book is dedicated to my husband, Alan Campbell Eachus, ACE. Without his steadfast confidence in this project, his research skills, and a computer moxie that far outstrips my own, this effort would never have gotten off the ground. Thank you for support, nurture, and encouragement. If there is any luster in this endeavor it comes from his polishing. Any errors I claim as my own.

Beauty

Better Than Right has grown my sense of beauty, of the little things, and of the seemingly little things that in truth are the really big things in life. One of my six roommates my sophomore year in college used to wake up on her top bunk and say, "It's a beautiful world." Finding beauty reveals a connection in such intricate patterns of mystery and support.

Community

This notion of community is most challenging to me. I seem to need to nail down community, but its currents are so fluid that they defy my need to catch them. Like the Holy Spirit, they blow where they will. My growing edge is to be present with them as they flow and blow. It is my hope that you who read my offering will find reminders of the appreciation, beauty and community that grow you.

EASY AS ABC

The Colon

Books that have a colon in the title intrigue me. There is so much gravitas on the right side of the colon. It is also a tip-off to the author's perspective. So my mental gymnastics were in Olympic form when I figured I, too, could have a colon in the title. *Better Than Right: ABC.*

While sloshing around in my creative juices, there seemed to be three components in *Better Than Right*. Identifying them would help the reader understand where I was coming from and where I hoped to go. Just using *ABC* in the title might pique interest too. I would divide the book into three segments: Appreciation, Beauty, and Community. This would be the terrain for sharing my hope that we can journey to a place that is much richer and more viable than being right.

I started gathering material, writing more, and envisioning those three divisions into which I would drop each article, and presto!—the book would lay itself out in three neat sections. I wrote the introductions for each.

Appreciation

I believe that appreciation is a holy thing—that when we look for what's best in a person we happen to be with at the moment, we're doing what

God does all the time. So in loving and appreciating our neighbor, we're participating in something sacred.

—Fred Rogers

It is often difficult for me to appreciate those who come into my purview and nudge me to move over on the bench to make room. I am not always enthralled by the people who are "riding the pines" with me, waiting for the coach to call them into the game. Yet babies know appreciation; their smiles are instantaneous. For me, it seems that appreciation comes in layers through repeated exposure, although it initially feels like a burr under the saddle.

It takes time to work things out, to figure out relationships, and to find thankfulness and appreciation for what others bring to the table. Appreciation, like pregnancy, is a growing adventure, calling for change and accommodation to see with God's eyes. I do not have the big picture, but I share from my primer on appreciation where faint glimmers reveal promise of something richer than being right.

Beauty

In his book *Seven Ways of Looking at Pointless Suffering: What Philosophy Can Tell Us about the Hardest Mystery of All*, Scott Samuelson looks at suffering from multiple religious and philosophical angles and finds that the misery of suffering defies meaning and convergence at a single response. The Enlightenment's response was "Fix it," yet relentless suffering litters our contemporary landscape. Suffering's prevalence has turned many to a different philosophical and religious response: "Face it." Samuelson says, "At its most inspired, we transform unjust suffering into profound art, culture, and knowledge, and elevate death and injustice in visions of beauty, adventure, and salvation."[1]

[1] Scott Samuelson, *Seven Ways of Looking at Pointless Suffering* (Chicago: University of Chicago Press, 2018) 7.

With our roots deep in the soil of suffering and pain, we cling to our humanity. We create. It is the poets, Samuelson observes, who help us hold on to our piece of the puzzle, claim it, and acknowledge others in their own corners doing the same thing while not staking out a one-size-fits-all response.

In this section on beauty, I note some of the ways beauty has crossed my path as I was aware enough at that juncture to name it.

Community

For all the gadgets we use and ways we are connected to each other, we are lonely people. "Community" is my takeaway from all the heartbreak, hatred, and oppression caused by the hemorrhage of human potential, despoiling of land and water, deprivation of freedom, illegal incarceration, violation of international law, and disregard for human values. These snapped into clear focus on my first trip to Palestine. Yet six years later, thinking that community was one of the legs that held up that fragile table seems ludicrous in the light of all that has happened since Pope Francis and I walked the land at the same time. Ah, but what is six years in the sweep of humanity?

In my small boat, community seems a land untenable. I have been buffeted by the winds of malevolence and greed. The words I have said so often as a pastor, "A table where all God's people can gather in peace," ring hollow and echo through canyons of brokenness and bitterness. It is hard to find the only thing left in Pandora's box: hope.

It may be time to turn my lens to a different length, a paradigm shift, even an intergalactic lens like the mystics, perhaps, who catch the glimmer of creation's readjustment to a cosmos-centric understanding of the expanding universe that includes all and lovingly gazes on each part of creation.

Warren Richey's book *Without a Paddle* described his race in a sea kayak around the state of Florida. In his lonely odyssey, I caught a glimmer of what might be an intermediate step for me in these rough seas. He writes:

> "There is a disconnect between modern American life and the natural world. Man is the most dangerous animal, with his ability to think, reason, and plan. But the greatest challenge isn't to fight the natural world, it is to find one's place in it. Human beings are not intended to walk the earth as omnipotent gods demanding that all other forms of life bow down. If the world is a perfectly balanced system, the place for man is a part of that system, not as the one who determines the balance. We are not the creator; we are part of the creation. To think otherwise is the worst kind of sacrilege. The most important lesson … is humility. It is achieving a kind of grace in a place of terror. Or at least trying. That's what it means to walk in grizzly country."[2]

He goes on to explain what grace in the face of terror looks like as he faces a storm:

> "I did not try to weigh the strength in my arm and my expertise in a kayak against the fury of the storm. This was not a mathematical calculation. I recognized this as a critical moment in my journey around Florida and perhaps the turning point in the Florida Challenge. It was not a question of my will or depth of my desire to reach Cedar Key that day. It would be wrong and dangerous to force my way into the storm. Instead of defiance, what I most needed was submission. Instead of personal willpower, what I needed was permission.

"Is the door open? May I proceed?

> "It is not about strength, or fancy paddlework, or even courage. It is about remaining faithful and obedient to the answer when it comes, whatever it might be … If I am faithful and obedient, I should have nothing to

[2] Warren Richey, *Without a Paddle* (NY: St. Martin's Press, 2010) 200.

> fear. In contrast, if I am willful and defiant and try to force my way through the storm, I would be on my own. That would be extraordinarily dangerous under those conditions."[3]

Like Richey as he contemplated heading into the storm, I need to ask permission, regain a true sense of who I am, and obediently proceed. Dr. Martin Luther King Jr. decided to turn back on "Bloody Sunday," March 7, 1965, at the Edward Pettus Bridge in Selma, Alabama, to avoid further violence. It was three weeks later that civil rights marchers crossed that bridge on their way to changing American history.

But I need to make a course correction. Community seems like nirvana right now, a faraway country. Companionship is the crutch that helps me limp along until I can get to community. I am like the pilgrims who travel to Santiago de Compostela, walking a while with one traveler before moving on in a different path or pace.

I still hope for community. I know it is there. Creation is made up of ecosystems that reveal our intricate and complex interrelatedness. For now, my route takes me through companionship, sharing, and learning. Using companionship, I look and long for community.

Help!

But my ABCs didn't work. I would put something I had written in one folder, then read it later only to decide it belonged in another folder. While the ABCs were descriptive, they did not differentiate. It was an alphabet soup, not three sides on the *Better Than Right* menu. The ABCs just didn't do it.

Part of the pandemic's fallout is that Americans are focusing more on cooking and learning to develop subtle palates. In much the same way, other categories that define existence need redefinition to capture life as it

[3] ibid., 287.

is lived today. The colon and the ABC, I discovered, are not fully refined. I was thrown back onto the starting blocks to describe that land my heart longs for—the faint land I glimpsed that beckons to me with winds that blow where they will and hint of a new day. I believe in my ABCs. But I have discovered that relationships are complex and not easily defined nor separated. They may be the subtle flavors and hints of flavor that we are yet learning to become accustomed.

As you journey with me, you will note that some titles begin with *Northern Gardener*. These are articles I wrote for a church newsletter in Hollywood, Florida. They are markers where I observed the unfolding of the mystery through gardening.

NORTHERN GARDENER

Shaved Sidewalks

The whole town of Niagara-on-the-Lake, Ontario is a glorious garden during the summer Shaw Festival! Imagine a city that employs six gardeners just to water the cascading hanging baskets and medians bursting with summer's blooms! Two things struck me while I was there. One, hope is a choice; and two, shaving sidewalks is how to build community.

I don't know if Niagara-on-the-Lake has exceptionally cold winters or winters prone to freezing and thawing. What I observed as I walked the quaint streets of this tourist city was that shaving sidewalks creates a way for us to navigate the garden easily. Think of it. When one section of sidewalk gets out of kilter from winter's heave or spring's rushing and burrowing waters, that block isn't consigned to the jackhammer and sledge as if some cosmic judge had found it unworthy at the bar of acceptable sidewalks. It isn't further broken and carried away to be ground and pulverized into a new attempt, one that will hopefully measure up. Oh no.

The community on the shores of Lake Ontario just north of Niagara Falls has decided that the strength of the many is maintained by helping those who fall out of alignment. Hence, when one block sinks beneath the others the neighboring sections are shaved down to meet it. The strong, standing in a smooth path, is shaped to help a section out of whack to enjoy life in the community again. When a concrete soldier suddenly rises out of step with the legion it is likewise rounded down to complete its mission, a smooth path for those who will follow. Like lighting a candle, one can light another, and neither is diminished. In this way, the offending concrete finds its place as a part of the purposeful path.

I wonder if there could be shaved sidewalks in the United States. Could there be places where a Muslim sidewalk, for example, isn't immediately suspected of terrorism if one corner seems to protrude at an uncomfortable angle for foot traffic? Could the toning down of blanket indictments and prejudices create a path where we could all walk together down the road to a future of hope and a community far better and more nurturing than the jackhammer's assault that seeks out deviants? Could first imagining other ways to the same destination reduce our resistances and prejudices? Would shaved corners of our rough edges make the beliefs of others more easily understood and accommodated? How could we begin to shave our disjointed places to strengthen the whole community instead of pointing fingers and living in fear? Could we be reshaped into a productive and flourishing village if we just possessed the largess to see it?

Elizabeth Barrett Browning, wrote:

> "Earth is crammed with heaven. Every common bush is alive with the fire of God. Only those who see take off their shoes. The rest sit around picking blackberries."[4]

The second thing I noted in Niagara-on-the-Lake was that hope was a choice. We saw the 1950 play, *Harvey*, about an invisible white rabbit which Elwood P. Dowd alone could see. When my husband selected the play I thought it a silly choice but against incredible odds white rabbit seekers and seers are also able to see as God sees---the possibilities deep within that are hidden from those who jackhammer sidewalks and take aim at the speck in their neighbor's eye. Elwood P. Dowd chose to see the fire alive in each of us and in his childlike naiveté and rather-high pitched voice he withstands the assaults of his sister and the world of reality and takes off his shoes and listens for hope spoken and received in humanity fairly expressed.

---

[4] Elizabeth Barrett Browning, *Aurora Leigh, Book 7.*

What strength of character it takes to live in hope, not succumbing to jadedness and bitterness! What resolve to tirelessly seek the shards of goodness that glint and glimmer within each of us. Resistance is pervasive. Common sense trumps perceived goodness. Very few have seen Harvey or the fiery common bush in its full color. Yet shaved sidewalks bear witness to the wisdom of communities that look within themselves and find ways make strong, supportive paths to the future.

IDENTITY THEFT

There is something comforting in knowing how universal temptation is. Even Jesus is tempted in the wilderness. Newly-minted in his baptism by water and the Holy Spirit, he is being test-marketed as the Son of Man, which is church talk for he is the real deal, fully human and fully divine. His first-round foe will be the devil.

In and of itself Jesus' adversary should be a tip-off that Jesus is a force to be reckoned with, for humankind is easily tripped up by shiny objects, no need to call the devil. Humans fall for the lazy way out, a little something extra "on the side," and turning a few heads never hurts. Jesus' temptation menu is bread from stones, power to make people BFFs and elevation to superhero, with jaw-dropping abilities like throwing yourself off tall buildings without even as much as scraping a toe in the landing---possessions, prestige, and power. What else is there really?

To repent in Hebrew means to turn around and walk the other way. It would be a hard sell for most of us if we sat down with our children and helped them map out their futures that didn't offer some combination of the big three offered to Jesus in the wilderness. When I was a teacher, I used to regularly ask the seventh and eighth graders to write about what they were going to do with your "one wild and precious life." They wanted to be doctors or lawyers because of the perks of the profession. The profession was a stepping stone, not to public service or improvement of our common lot, but to a red sports car or a condo in a high rise with waterfront views downtown. They have fallen for what is idealized on their own personal window to the world. To be fair, some students in the back row would align themselves with careers in sports, performance or the arts where the reverence of stardom would celebrate their uniqueness. And there would always be those quiet ones who never would volunteer an opinion. They were taking it all in and processing it through their nascent filters of the ways of the world.

The Epistle of First John in the New Testament offers an alternative world view to that embraced by my seventh and eighth graders. Around the end of the first century, in a very turbulent time, there was dissension among the early Christians. They were arguing over a question that history hasn't found a solution: who is Jesus? First John 3:1-3 NSRV offers these words:

> See what love the Father has given us, that we should be called children of God; and that is what we are. The reason that the world does not know us is that it did not know him. Beloved, we are God's children now; what we will be has not yet been revealed. What we do know is this; when he is revealed, we will be like him, for we will see him as he is. And all who have this hope in him purify themselves, just as he is pure.

The prerequisite is to know *whose* we are. The careful self-definition of "I am this, not that," doesn't lead to understanding of our larger identity. We see the pain of this extreme isolation and hatred of otherness that leads to violent eruptions with less warning than a volcano. Starting with "I, me, my, mine" produces a grain of sand with no comprehension of the shore. The first letter of John says first we are in relationship with God, God's choice, we've been claimed as beloved children. We understand 13.8 billion years began with a Creator whose unfolding initiative is the impetus for shaping us into God's beloved children. Our relational life force grows us into its likeness of the Prime Mover, "for where your treasure is, there also is your heart (Mt 6:21 NRSV)." My young students were striking out alone but in time they may see intricacies of the vast relationships as we honor the ever-expanding knowledge of the web of life. This web of life seems antithetical to the offerings of the devil---power, possessions and prestige---goals for the self. Yet even unknowingly, their identity has been stolen. The lures of the world pull them to DIY quick fixes and face lifts. Patience, wisdom and courage to discover the beauty of true identity in relationship with the one who loved us first would be a long haul.

The Long Road

Gaining true identity, while hardly enticing, does offer some benefits: it is time consuming, costly, and offers breath-taking views of the previously-undiscovered treasures. It kindles creative fires within. It usually begins with laundry lists of the out-of-kilter, stacks of incomplete and not-worth-it tasks piled helter-skelter, a gnawing sense of incompleteness, a cynicism that is hidden in plain sight like the toxic lead in Flint, Michigan's drinking water.

The process is counter-intuitive. The cure for "I, me, my, mine" is to look intently within. We must gaze into it, to know the files of perceived slights and insults, the catalogs of the failures of others, and to lament the world's blindness. This takes time. And then running and rerunning these films in the theatre of our mind can fill hours with sanctimonious self-righteousness and the agony of isolation, or litanies of "I'm not good enough." Like being on quicksand we must lie flat across it if we hope to free ourselves from the sucking whoosh of our perceived goodness. The danger is that the next field of quicksand looks pretty much like regular sand until you have stepped on it.

Counselors and spiritual directors spend hours in the labyrinths of agony as clients try to reorient their lives to the one who calls them beloved. Hercules found the Augean stables were full and needed a good flush. It changed the course of a river. It changed Hercules. The time-consuming task of living with the accumulated debris of our past needs a heavy dose of reality, but it can change our lives.

Marie Kondo's 2014 book, *The Life Changing Magic of Tidying Up,* brought a fresh approach to our over-consumptive habits. The book caused such a revelation in the house and heart of one of my friends that she completely reorganized her home and reoriented her life. The author says that mindset is the cornerstone of the process. The goal is a positive relationship with the things that bring us joy. We need to get rid of what is no longer needed in our lives. Thank it for being a part of our lives and let go.[5]

Richard Rohr, in *Falling Upward*, tells of the dismissing the faithful soldier in Japan. Soldiers were soldiers "til death do us part" or they fell on their swords, whichever happened first. Following the WW II there was no longer going to be a militarized Japan and soldiers needed to "get a life." The ritual of dismissing the soldier was the gathering the family, friends and neighbors of the soldier and recalling all the bravery and steadfastness of the soldier. No small act of courage was too small to mention. At the end of the ceremony as the soldier was bathed in recognition of his deeds and valor, he received a harsh slap across the face and was told to make a new life. The slap was a releasing of the past that served so well; it was vivid welcome to a world that no longer needed his soldiering.[6]

WIN or WAN?

Football players who come down the tunnel at Notre Dame stadium slap a sign above the entranceway as they go out onto the field. It simply says, "What's Important Now," and its acronym, WIN, focuses the players on what is next. A Maria Kondo follower tells of her struggle to keep things tidy after the joyful purge of her clutter. Try as she might she just couldn't get the hang of picking up the stray pencil or sock until she joined the football players and focused her attention on the present moment, What About Now, or WAN, became her mantra as she encountered creeping clutter in her organized home. Being present in the moment is the way to move forward. It may take a long time before the beginning regimen becomes a habit of an uncluttered heart. But Christ too is evolving from a Western intellectual *tour de force* that is logical, abstract, privatized and individualized into a new understanding of Christ amid diversity and

---

[5] Marie Kondo, *The Life Changing Magic of Tidying Up* (Berkeley, CA: Ten Speed Press, 2014).

[6] Richard Rohr, *Falling Upward* (San Francisco: Jossey-Bass, 2011) 43-44.

difference, celebrating uniqueness and energy integral to understanding ourselves, and others in the emerging meaning of the cosmic Christ.

First A Word

We have tended to think of Christ as Jesus' last name much like Catholics choose a saint's name to add to their own when they are confirmed. But our identity is not an individual exercise to finally arrive at ground zero where we will make our "Here I Stand" declaration with Martin Luther. Our identity is a shared understanding that we are God's children and that identity has not yet been fully revealed. Our hope is that by consciously choosing Jesus Christ, we will move toward deep unity with God. To bear that witness is to become a source of healing for the sake of the community.

Ilia Delio writes, "We must *choose to be whole*, to be attentive to God's ongoing work in our lives. God will not create a new future for us, but God invites us to become more whole *within* ourselves so that we may become more whole *among* ourselves. Evolution toward greater wholeness is evolution toward more life and love. This is the basis of contemplative evolution and the emergence of Christ."[7]

She explained, "Christ is the power of God among us and within us, the fullness of the earth and of life in the universe. We humans have the potential to make Christ alive; it is what we are created for. To live the mystery of Christ is not to speak about Christ but to live in the surrender of love, the poverty of being, and the cave of the heart. If we can allow the Spirit to really take hold of us and liberate us from our fears, anxieties, demands, and desire for power and control, then we can truly…live in the risen Christ who empowers us to build this new creation."[8]

---

[7] Ilia Delio, *The Unbearable Wholeness of Being: God, Evolution and the Power of Love* (Maryknoll, NY: Orbis Books, 2013) 202-203.

[8] Ilia Delio, *Christ in Evolution*. (Maryknoll, NY: Orbis Books, 2008) 180.

What's Happening in Our Time

It seems counter-intuitive that our identity has been stolen when we don't even know our truest self. The first developmental task Maslow tells us to learn to trust. But knowing and trusting ourselves does not happen in a vacuum. It is a lifelong journey. We are shaped by our culture, a rapidly changing culture, as you well know when you call a grandchild to help with a computer problem

Matthew Fox looks at our time and sees our identity theft comes from our failure to recognize and claim what is sacred, namely our earth home. He quotes Thomas Berry, prophetic environmentalist, "As absence of the sacred is the most basic flaw in many of our efforts at ecologically or environmentally adjusting our human presence to the natural world. It has been said, 'we will not save what we do not love' but it is also true that we will neither love nor save what we do not experience as sacred. Eventually only our sense of sacred will save us."[9]

We can no longer look at coral reefs dying, for example, a dead pregnant sperm whale washed ashore with 48 pounds of plastic in her gut off Sardinia, in a marine sanctuary created for dolphins and whales and claim there is no environmental crisis.[10]

To deny something important is a moral outrage. Denial then cuts us off from what we know is good. We are called to do something about this loss of goodness or we create shibboleths of smaller consequences to obsess about. We have become fearful people. While it is good to know boundaries, fear plays into the hands of those who use it against us. They assure us of their answers to the myriad of complex problems while, uncertain we wring our hands awash in acedia and despair. That fear has

---

[9] Matthew Fox Commencement Address, Oberlin College 2019. Thomas Berry quote from *Tikken Magazine,* "Developing Environmental Consciousness," June 25, 2019.

[10] Alejandra Borunda, "The Mediterranean Sea Is Choked with Plastic Waste; Sperm Whale Is Latest Casualty," *The Miami Herald,* April 2, 2019, A14.

immobilized us, we do not gain any traction to move forward. How can we possibly find our identity when we are looking over our shoulder?

Fools Rush In

Yet there are fools who watch the chaos and see in the center of the turmoil dancing rays of light. Howard Thurmond saw it in Jesus and the disinherited in Palestine in the first century CE. Rabbi Abraham Herschel saw it in the ancient prophets of Israel whose words are full of the absolute wonder of creation and the ability of humankind to do the work of God. Their lenses tracked a movement barely perceptible. Claiming to be beloved children of God whose identity may not yet be fully revealed, fools shine their light to help others claim their identity.

They look to see where the kingdom of God is at hand. Elwin Wilson gained his true identity when several events converged in his life. It was 2009 and Barack Obama had just been elected president. A friend asked him if he were to die right now, where you would go and Wilson replied to hell, for Wilson was troubled about his past.[11]

In the spring of 1961 Freedom Riders arrived at the Greyhound Bus station in Rock Hill, South Carolina, to integrate bus station waiting rooms in the South. Wilson and a group of young white men attacked and savagely beat a white man, Albert Bigelow, and an African American man, John R. Lewis at the station. The men did not fight back. They never pressed charges for they were non-violent protestors. Wilson also took part in attacks against civil rights workers at lunch counter sit-ins. Wilson never knew the names of those whom he attacked.

But 46 years later Wilson contacted the *Rock Hill Herald* to research the names of those whom he had injured. He was amazed that one of them had become a US Congressperson. He then traveled to Washington, DC, to ask John R. Lewis, representative from Georgia, to forgive him. Lewis

[11] "Elwin Wilson, Who Apologized for Racists Acts Dies at 76," *The New York Times*, April 1, 2013, A16.

neither knew the names nor remembered their faces of his assailants. Rather he devoted his lifetime to changing the America's condoning and looking away from the evils of racism.

When Wilson met Lewis they celebrated their common humanity and they both cried. Lewis' forgiveness was healing for them both. "Hate is too heavy a burden to carry," Rep. Lewis said as they enjoyed the harvest of nonviolence 46 years later. Lewis said he never remembered the faces of those who abused him but he would never forgot the first man who came to ask for his forgiveness. After his Washington visit, Wilson felt like he had just apologized to the whole world and it felt good.[12]

After the televised interview Wilson received an irate phone call from a young man screaming that he had broken his Ku Klux Klan promise of 1961. Wilson said his father had told him that a wise man changes his mind, a fool never. He hoped the young man would be able to get rid of his hate.

Twenty-one centuries ago, someone who devoted his life to nonviolence, remarked, "There is more joy in heaven over one sinner who repents than over ninety-nine righteous persons who need no repentance" (Lk 15:7 NRSV). Gaining our rightful identity may take a lifetime.

---

[12] https://www.sandiegouniontribune.com/sdut-segregationist-apology-020509-2009feb05-story.html

ROAD MAPS

Road maps are almost passé. We simply hit the touchscreens in our car, check a Google map or Waze and off we go, trusting. But most of us have life road maps in our heads. We learned about them at our parents' knee, what education we need, values to foster and what makes a successful life. We learn about rough patches and detours from our family of origin. We have it all laid out until the road washes out, a bridge collapses or a new interstate is built. Then our maps are inadequate. We find ourselves at a great divide and we will need new strategies if we are to continue.

Kate Bowler was a thirty-five-old professor of American Christian history at Duke University Divinity School when her road washed out. Kate's research focused on the Prosperity Gospel, championed by those who believe that God wants you to be successful in this world. Material blessings and well-being are confirmation that your faith is strong enough and you are proceeding faithfully. Less than that is a call to examine your faith.

Awful Irony

Imagine her surprise and the enormous irony, when this professor, wife, and mother of a toddler was diagnosed with stage IV cancer in 2015. She had sat in the pews, listened, and studied the Prosperity Gospel for ten years. It had been her life's work. She wrote her doctoral thesis about it and came to know this arm of Christianity intimately, never reduced it to caricature. She found it had a kind of tenacity that God would make a way no matter what. While Kate acknowledges it is easy to get lost in the Prosperity Gospel's absurdity, she found a resilient hope that their circumstances would not define them. God has a better way. [13]

Now Kate found herself the one being examined. She wondered about her faith. A researcher, but not a proponent of the Prosperity Gospel, she now had a lot of time to reflect during her "enduring purgatory," the dreadful journey of her illness.[14] She was critically ill, suffering through surgeries, hospital stays, needles, and prolonged recuperation while watching her life twist, contort and diminish helplessly. She was struck with the irony of her faith in the light of her life's work. She began writing her story for the *New York Times*[15] and people responded through the lens of their experiences. Bowler was dealing with who she was when her road map was useless.

Critical Junctions, New Realizations

Every day consciously or unconsciously, we make assumptions about our life map. Most of us have felt some twinge of upheaval physically, politically, economically, ecologically, socially, or spiritually. In her anxious time, road map gone, Kate assumed her plucky attitude and can-do spirit would lead her to imagined life. She was not prepared for the ensuing reality.

We can relate to the insecurity and feeling ill-prepared when the map is useless. How do we move forward with freedom and grace while feeling increasingly apprehensive about so many aspects of our lives? Will we be tripped up by a health crisis? Will a sustaining relationship be broken? Will our identity be stolen? Our private lives dragged into the public sphere and there distorted? Where is our faith? We also worry about the groups to which we have given our allegiance. Fearful, we are left with inadequate maps and new terrains to be crossed.

---

[13] Faith and Leadership.com, Episode 5 podcast reprint: Kate Bowler on the presence of God in the face of death, January 28, 2018, 8.

[14] ibid., 5.

[15] Kate Bowler, "Death, the Prosperity Gospel and Me," *New York Times* Op Ed February 13, 2016.

Kate Bowler discovered in her new times she had no road map; everything was called into question. She discovered:

1. plucky good will and stamina wouldn't insure she get through;
2. she was special and important to God, which is like everybody's specialness with God;
3. the good life is not a reward;
4. choosing the right doesn't guarantee that there will be no push back or huge bumps;
5. she was unable to make sense of her life; she was not the architect of life.[16]

What's Next after No

Old assumptions do not hold in new time. We do not recognize the landscape. The Beatitudes begin this way: You are blessed when you are at the end of your rope. With less of you there is more of God and his rule. (Mt 5:3, *The MSG*).

Less of us, more of God? Is that where we are? Have we gotten too comfortable? We have gotten good at the usual, the expected, the traditional way. We are less stellar when it comes to change, but it is not our foible exclusively. Change puts many in a place where comfort must be abandoned, uncomfortable things tolerated, visions altered, expectations changed, and losses grieved. Without a road map, we come face-to-face with the knowledge that we are too weak to change the powers, principalities, and cosmic forces. Rugged individualism crumbling, we are in too much disarray to heal our painfully broken hearts.

Going Off the Grid

Kate's notion used to be that life was a basket in which she was to cram as many of her expectations of life as possible--- a fulfilling career, an enduring and endearing relationship with her spouse, and colleagues and

[16] ibid., 9.

students who delighted in her, and children whom she had protected and guided. She was the chief architect of that vision.[17]

Many of us have that basket mentality too---we want lives full of cherished fulfillment. When we set ourselves up to think we deserve or expect certain things to happen, we are setting ourselves up for constant unhappiness and an inability to allow what is going to happen anyway to happen. Rigid and fearful we resist almost everything. But one of the paradoxes of having no map is the road through giving up control is marked with compassion and understanding, union, and an introduction to the final letting go, death.

We have been schooled in letting go as we have faced social restrictions, economic insecurity and fear our bodies will not stand up to the assault of a new enemy, a virus that looks like a milkweed blossom.

Kate has written a book entitled *Everything Happens for a Reason and Other Lies I Have Loved.*[18] She explained her former road map is no longer descriptive of her life. She is setting horizons in a different way, living life intentionally. In coming to the end of basket mentality she came to the place where God begins, where God does the resurrection thing, and life takes on true beauty in ways that are not our ways. It is not about surrendering, giving up, capitulating, or stopping planning and thinking; it is keeping living water flowing through us. This surrender takes us to where peacefulness flows into love, letting go of the self and finding you have been sheltered in the Self all along.

Kate said it well, "I discovered the best part of me was not me, but where I end, God begins."[19] We are challenged by life's unyielding circumstances. We sit with the painful choices and claim only our uncertainty. But God begins, "and I am still baffled that this terrible time has been the most important time of my life, that everything felt brand-new again. And so in the midst of the terrible hospital world and needles, there was always

---

[17] ibid., 10.

[18] Kate Bowler, *Everything Happens for a Reason and Other Lies I have Loved* (NY: Random House, 2018).

[19] "Death, the Prosperity Gospel and Me" 10.

the sense that God can make things new with or without me, and I think that's a lesson I'll have to relearn again and again."[20]

With our road maps archaic, God moves us to new vistas of God's saving power. And like Kate Bowler, we move ahead one day at a time, uncertain of outcomes, often worn and frazzled, but confident that where we end, God begins, and that is the best part of us. That is where we are. Check your GPS. We are coming home.

[20] Ibid., 11.

NOT ALL CIRCLES ARE ROUND

The basest of all things is to be afraid.
---William Faulkner

My friend, Caroline Cracraft, invited me to go to Palestine with a group of church women in 2014. Interested but fearful, because since childhood I believed Palestine and Israel in the same sentence were synonymous with violence. It took a great deal of inner dialogue before I plopped down my deposit and looked at the requirements for travel in Israel. My reading and prayer had not prepared me for what I would experience as a first-time traveler in what is euphemistically called the Holy Land. Looking back, that trip has become a metaphor for the unfolding of my life since then. What little I knew, those specks of information, conjectures, Sunday School images, seminary training and feelings would meet the reality of boots on the ground and increase, modify or blow out of the water most of the things I had thought were true of Palestine. It changed my world.

On our trip between the river and the sea, we traveled in Palestinian buses, stayed in Palestinian hotels, and heard Jewish, Christian and Muslim speakers tell what they were doing to bring cooperation, peace, and the end of a brutal apartheid. This trip had the feeling of intrigue for we were told to be careful what sort of literature we brought into the country. We didn't get any itinerary until the group met in Bethlehem and it was parceled out daily lest we inadvertently compromise our Palestinian friends.

Women of the Abrahamic faiths told how they worked to foster cooperation, understanding and hasten the end of a brutal system that distorts both the oppressor and the oppressed. Partnering with others or creating their own organization they sought to do their part to find a common ground, a path through the morass that deeply touches those who live in Israel, the Middle East, and the United States.

The Elephant in the Living Room

I tried to reconcile what I had heard most of my life with what we saw and heard---woman after woman spoke to their reality of Palestine, and their work to breach the walls that separate people and cultures based on hatred and fear and forced isolation that distorts. For example, we met Vera Baboun, the mayor of Bethlehem, whose husband spoke out against injustices and imprisonment of Palestinians without due process. He was imprisoned, without due process, only released when he was a broken and ill man. She continued his fight and served as mayor of Bethlehem from 2012 to 2017. She welcomed the Pope and the faithful who sang "O Come All You Faithful" and "Angels We Have Heard on High" filling Bethlehem Square with their voices of pain and hope in 2014. A time of hope in a lopsided circle.

Susan Sahouri of the Bethlehem Fair Trade Artisans told us that hope changes as the situation on the ground changes. Coming to Palestine from Germany after the second Intifada, Susan led the fair trade artisans. In 2014 all she had was a staff of two Palestinian women and ten international volunteers. With a small database, a fair-trade website, they began to sell exquisite handmade embroidered wall hangings, paraments, and table linens, and wooden artifacts made from the olive wood all created by local artists. The fair traders also sell and export olive oil from their 50 producers. This is incredibly important because of the huge obstacles and delays that the Israelis place on getting any Palestinian goods out of Israel.

The Separation Wall, built through Bethlehem in 2003 through 2008, divides the city from the surrounding desert of oppression and a sea of salt. Susan reminded us it does what it was built it for: Palestinians can't get to their jobs, further weakening the economy and increasing unemployment. They are further cut off from each other and Israel. They must drive many extra miles further to get between places. Work being done by the artisans offers a ray of hope that the Palestinian economy could someday bloom in the desert of oppression around the sea. Wholeness is a circle where each can contribute to the dance of life. Life in Israel is distorted circles rolling in their drunken manner toward the brink of calamity.

John Phillip Newell wrote:

> "If the deep spirit of our age is this new awareness of life's essential oneness, if the new Pentecost is leading us into what David Bohm calls a 'non-fragmentary world view,' then what are we to make of deep fragmentation of the world today? What is it that is driving humanity to the precipitous edge of self-destruction, more dangerous than anything history has witnessed? At the heart of our fragmentation, whether as nations and wisdom traditions or as races and societies, are various forms of fundamentalism...By fundamentalism I mean any system that perceives reality in hard-edged terms, that boxes in truth with four fixed walls of definition.
>
> "At the heart of such hard-edged boundaries is fear. Fundamentalism has always reared its head at times of significant change. Think, for instance, of the extreme fundamentalisms that came to expression in the Christian household in the nineteenth century---biblical literalism at one end of the transition. Fundamentalism reacted to the spirit of the age by further hardening in lines of definition and by trying to impose rigid boundaries on the emerging future... We too live in the midst of enormous change.[21]

The Palestinian and Israeli women, Christian, Jewish, and Muslim, were determined to speak truth to power. Despite all they had experienced, they believed that justice brings peace, and that violence perpetuates violence.

---

[21] John Phillip Newell, *New Harmony: The Spirit, the Earth, and the Human Soul,* (San Francisco: Jossey-Bass, 2011), prologue xv-xvi.

To win you must love. The Palestinian women work for a pittance, often because the men in their family can find no work.

Jewish and Palestinian women work together to change hearts and secure a better tomorrow for the teenagers of the land. Kids 4 Peace takes a like number of Israeli and Palestinian boys and girls and sends them for a summer experience which opens eyes and transforms hearts as they explore each other's cultures. Those slots are highly competitive, and there is a yearlong orientation before they can experience living together as equals. The slots are highly sought, especially by Palestinian girls.

The Palestinian women served us dinner and told their stories in the hope that when we returned to the United States, we would become ambassadors for justice with peace in their time, in their land. They live in dusty, run-down cities, lacking electricity, where water is turned off for days and weeks at a time, while gleaming illegal settlements with well-watered lawns sprout upon their ancestral homelands. They watch as their olive trees are cut down or bulldozed by a hostile army and settlers, their children maimed when they participate in Friday freedom marches. They have been turned away at checkpoints that provide access to jobs, education, health care or even a trip to the beach. They must travel on different roads, decrepit roads, while the Israeli infrastructure provides superhighways from the big cities to the illegal settlements for a quick commute for those with the coveted yellow Israeli license plates.

The international community has only minimally addressed the problem of the Palestinian/Israeli conflict. Arab and Israeli supporters have not hammered out even a rudimentary definition of parameters of the problem. The Palestinian leadership is as divided as the West Bank is from Gaza. For over 100 years there has been no acknowledgement of Britain's broken promise in the Balfour Accords which contained two promises: one, the "establishment in Palestine of a national home for the Jewish people," and two," it clearly be understood that nothing shall be done which may prejudice the civil and religious rights of existing non-Jewish communities in Palestine..." The Rev. Robert Assaly, a member of the Churches Middle East Working Group, calls the Balfour declaration, "the Middle East's original sin." Yet on the centenary anniversary, November 2017 Prime Ministers Theresa May and Benjamin Netanyahu marked the occasion with a London dinner party at the home of the current Lord Balfour. It seems endless. While the elephant sits and grows unmolested in the living room, we are caught in a hamster wheel, tumbled, bruised, disoriented. Or are we?

A New Earth

Ken Wilber's Integral Theory offers a respite from the angst and despair of this decline into chaos. It suggests rather than looking for the problem we seek all the parts of the whole. Just as Psychiatrist Murray Bowen didn't focus on the "identified client" but studied family systems, Integral Theory isn't as concerned with what's wrong, who's responsible, and whom we label "enemy." The Integral Theory looks at the entire family system, beginning at a new point, with different information and data.

Integral Method questions may feel as foreign as the scientific methodology felt 300 years ago. For the scientific method worked on the notion of analysis and diagnosis into constituent parts to discover what was wrong and how to fix it. The scientific method created winners and losers. Wilber's Integral Method begins by validating and connecting, looking for all the parts of the puzzle, what wholeness might be, the integration of synthesis and epistemological reality bringing together the inherent whole metaphysical and material worlds. This is a world as it appears without limits or boundaries, the world of matter and spirit, a world without boundaries of past and present which is fundamentally an enlarging and expanding of one's horizons, a growth outwardly in perspective and inwardly in depth.[22]

What does this theory have to do with Palestinian women working in a system of incredible oppression and ever-decreasing resources? Not all circles are round. We do not always know exactly at what point we are standing on a circle. We have been circling most of our lives. Straight

[22] Ken Wilber, *No Boundary*, (Boulder: Shambhala, 2001), chapter 3.

lines are for rulers. We have trudged for so long that it seems that the circle is bigger than we can comprehend, or we have inadvertently slipped off onto another circle. The women in Palestine I met are committed to love despite the brutality of their situation and the land grabs of illegal settlements by those Holocaust survivors who cry, "Never again," as the Israeli government squeezes life from the Palestinians one house at a time, one illegal settlement after another. History requires both remembering *and* connecting the dots.

Corralling all fragments of this intractable problem seems insurmountable. But another look at Wilber's Integral Theory says that changing the starting point even slightly leads to significantly different outcomes. Instead of current rhetoric which claims others are misguided, confused, infantile, or just plain wrong, Integral Method believes that there was some significance in previous levels of experience.[23]

The Franciscan priest Richard Rohr describes the phenomenon as using the third way, avoiding dualistic thinking of matter *or* spirit, conceiving both as an inseparable unity. The assumption of goodness within the fractures and upheaval is nothing short of bringing the Divine Spirit into our physical world, our place on the circle.[24]

Chaos is not random, there is order and pattern, Edward Lorenz asserted. But it is terribly difficult to predict. As a meteorologist he realized even small differences in a dynamic system could trigger vast and unsuspected results. His paper, "Predictability: Does the Flap of a Butterfly's Wings in Brazil Set Off a Tornado in Texas?" birthed not only the chaos theory but the butterfly effect. In terms of the Palestinian women in so great an arena, with so many players and so much confusion their insistence on respect for themselves and their commitment not to repay evil with evil, even

---

[23] _________, *Integral Meditation* (Boulder: Shambhala, 2016), 72.

[24] Richard Rohr, *Eager to Love*, (Cincinnati: Franciscan Media, 2014) 226-227.

honoring the enemy with respect and non-violence could be the butterfly effect, the slight change that brings greatly different results.[25]

The refugee crisis not only includes the refugee camps in the West Bank, Gaza and East Jerusalem in Israel but spills over into Jordan, Lebanon, and Syria. The result of the conflict of June 1946 to May 1948 was 550,000 refugees. Today there are 5,000,000 Palestinian refugees. (It is interesting to compare that with the number of the Jewish victims of the Holocaust, 6,000,000.) Many families have been refugees since 1948. As the Palestinian lands in Israel shrink with illegal settlements and a wall built on Palestinian land, Palestinian residents in Jerusalem cannot leave their home for even a few hours for fear the government will come in and seize their home as "abandoned" and install Jewish settlers there. Waving blue and white Israeli flags from windows signals that another Palestinian home has been confiscated by the Israelis. One-third of the Palestinian refugees live in the camps. The remaining two-thirds live around cities and towns in Jordan, Lebanon, the Syrian Arab Republic, and the West Bank, Gaza and East Jerusalem.

Life in a Hamster Cage

The aftermath of the 1967 Six Day War and Israeli Occupation of Palestine created ten more camps for refugee and non-refugee Palestinians. These camps while on host government land, are designated for United Nations Relief Works Agency (UNRWA) administration which provides services of schools, health and distribution centers. UNRWA also updates refugee records and receives refugee concerns and petitions. The conditions in the camps are deplorable, an infrastructure of dusty, crumbling streets, sewers, and sanitation conditions substandard. UNRWA does not police the area. For example, the refugees in Shuafat refugee camp pay the same East Jerusalem taxes as the residents of East Jerusalem but they receive rare

[25] Edward Lorenz, "Predictability: Does the Flap of a Butterfly's Wings in Brazil Set Off a Tornado in Texas?" *American Association for the Advancement of Science,* Washington, 1972. It has since been asserted that the 20th century will be remembered for three scientific revolutions---relativity, quantum mechanics and chaos.

garbage collection, little or no police protection, and emergency services that are so slow they are a joke. To enter the Shuafat refugee camp through its only ingress one must walk past overflowing dumpsters reeking with the stench of rotting garbage and Clorox. Some of the twenty-six thousand residents have taken to burning their garbage thus creating a health hazard of the toxic fumes.

Social workers from England were also visiting Shuafat when Caroline and I were there in May 2014. Specifically, they were looking at how the conditions of the refugee camp were contributing to the breakdown in social fiber of those trapped inside. For example, just outside the Shuafat refugee camp is a drug house which is called "Chicago East." Thirty to forty East Jerusalem police and the IDF doing their compulsory military service mill around their guard station turning a blind eye to the drug dealing next door. The drug trade further weakens the Palestinian social fiber for those trapped in the cage called Shuafat Refugee Camp.

Speaking Truth to Power

I met American born Sam Bahour on both trips to Palestine. A redwood of a man, he speaks eloquently and pragmatically. His story is that of an immigrant family who taught their son the story of their neighbors in El-Bireh, Palestine. He knew more about them than his neighbors in Youngstown, Ohio.

His passion was shaped by two horrific events. The first was the massacres of the Sabra and Shatila Refugee Camps in Lebanon by the Lebanese Christian militias after the 1982 Israeli invasion of Lebanon. These massacres would not have been possible without that Israeli invasion. The Lebanese Christian militia, Phalange, attacked the camps slaughtering 2,000 Palestinian refugees from September 16-18, 1982. The second event was the First Intifada in 1987-1988. Bahour is very aware that the US supports Israel with huge military funding yearly and casts its veto vote in the United Nations Security Council with Israel with knee-jerk regularity.

A successful Palestinian businessman, Bahour brought the first and largest communications company to Palestine. He then went on to build the first shopping mall in Ramallah, the quasi-capital of Palestine. Sam believes that Israel, after creating a strong state, should have put Zionism in a museum and cherished it for it served the state well.[26] Instead it rolled Zionism into every facet of the state. Fast forward to today and when Israel looks in a mirror and it sees Zionism in all phases of life. The butterfly effect says the slightest change brings greatly different results. Having endured a fifty-year occupation and subjugation of the apartheid it is time to claim what has been done. If they are true to Zionist ideology, with its exclusive definition, the conflict will continue, perpetuating an endless cycle of pain in this land. Zionism has the feel of a ball rolling with increasing velocity off a mountainside hurtling into darkness. The catastrophic results will stretch far into the future.

Expanding the Circle

Bahour now spends his time trying to develop the Palestinian economy through the international business community. Palestine has the resources to become a burgeoning economy needing only the international business partners to tap their potential, creating markets for their goods, and thus put pressure on Israel to change its death grip on Palestinian business and flow of capital and goods. Bahour shares his vision for progress in Palestine cogently, forcefully and with great passion. Moving solutions out of the political sphere creates new possibilities.

Some circles are inhabited by those who try to crowd others out. It is always a difficult task to try to figure out exactly where we are standing. Pushing and shoving seems endemic. Sometimes we get turned around or wander off like stray sheep. The Palestinian women I met continue to witness even as it seems futile or naïve, in a world gone mad with power and desire to control.

---

[26] Sam Bahour, "Listening Closely," *The Jerusalem Post Magazine*. August 11, 2017.

Distorted circles like amoebas, move in to devour. Illegal settlements surround Palestinian land, voices become fainter. Yet the Integral Method leaves nothing out: the spiritual underpinnings, the love for this rugged and fertile land, the histories of those who claim this land, their relationships with the nations that share Mediterranean Sea and its rugged land, all of it must be included, must be brought to the table. This method includes the great suffering, promises made and promises denied, all the physical, material and spiritual dimensions of this intractable problem and holds them all in a misshapen circle, watching, listening and waiting.

The mystics call this the third way. Here God is found in our imperfection and non-judgmental attitude which transforms us. Isn't that the story from this land on the first Easter? From our place on the circle, we sense a unity. Dualistic thinking has created an illusion. Spiritual awareness heightens our consciousness, and we intuit a *weltanschauung*, a worldview that encompasses all, for all are part of the creation in love. Is this what the Palestinian women and those who work tirelessly for peace see? The Integral Method says all the participants are included. While absorbed on this intractable problem the milieu changes.

There are questions in the air. Are we going forward armed only with the tools of the Enlightenment or is there a new breeze blowing of our time? Can the story of one change the heart of another? Of many? Has post-modernism's focus on experience brought us to the place where God's story and our story intersect, and we recognize both as sacred?

Marianne Borg, widow of New Testament scholar Marcus Borg hosts a monthly Zoom gathering entitled "Going Home *to* a New Way." She contends that "theopoetics" will be the way forward. God's revelation through poetic expression participates in the unfolding of the divine-human intersection. Answers will emerge that will crack the fear of fundamentalism: not by arm wrestling to conquer, not shouting over to subdue, but by recognizing humanity in the context of the goodness in our luminous and good creation in a cosmos which long ago was pronounced good.

The Whole Earth Round

Al Gore discussed our ecological predicament in *Hemispheres* magazine, July 2017.[27] He ended his interview with three quotes, all of which address the quandary of our world where few circles reflect the fullness and well-being of creation. Gore's quotes address the Palestinian women's concerns as well as the sacredness of Mother Earth. They help us keep our bearing to continue going forward, breathing life into the hope that we may be a part of adding fullness to the wholeness that creation intends. Gore quoted Nelson Mandela who said, "It's always impossible until it's done." In circles of life the uncertainty of our position keeps us open to the possibility that help is at hand, as Jesus reminds us that is where the kingdom of God is.

Like the fall of the Berlin Wall in 1989 there comes a moment of mystical opportunity for justice. Poet Wallace Stevens said, "After the final no there comes a yes/And on that yes the future world depends."[28] Learning to be at home in our circle suggests vigilance. We do not know the moment when the third way will emerge, or where or how the Integral Method will lead us to the butterfly effect: the home for which we long.

The late economist Rudi Dornbusch said: "Things take longer to happen than you think they will, and then they happen faster than you ever thought they could."[29] The Palestinian women live into *Zeitgeist,* the spirit of the age, and every day by their lives they commit themselves to the healing of the land they call home.

Not all circles are round. Finding the third way, a commitment to inclusion, may shape tomorrow far differently than we have imagined, by first shaping us!

---

[27] Bill Mc Kibbon, "The Crusade Continues," *Hemispheres,* July 2017, 47-50.

[28] Wallace Stevens, "The Well-Dressed Man with a Beard," *Selected Poems.* (New York: Alfred Knopf, 2009), 147.

[29] Rudi Dornbusch, US Congress, Senate Committee on the Budget (2012). *Concurrent Resolution on the Budget Fiscal Year 2013.* 95.

NORTHERN GARDENER

Not What We Expected

As my husband and I flew back to Illinois in late April visions of forsythia and tulips danced in my head. Reality quickly set in as fierce winter winds had pruned the soft maples in the back yard unceremoniously dumping big branches, really big branches, and sticks, everywhere in the back yard and a few on the roof of the house and garage. Not wanting us to feel lonely, neighbors' trees added more branches across our domain. Suitcases inside the door, we began stacking and breaking the branches up into what would become five bags of yard waste. Rubbing our achy backs, we looked at the leaves that had filled the flowers beds and borders and knew our next task, but we took a break. While we were gone the front garden had popped up with a colorful welcome for us.

But then…the weather forecast predicted---SNOW! It was thick, gloppy snow! Holding my cup of tea, I looked out on shivering and shriveling daffodils, and tulips nodding their red heads under the weight of the white stuff. The grape hyacinths, skinny and stiff in their purple and light blue bells kept a stiff upper lip. One would think it was too late for snow even in Illinois on April 25. We had planned to avoid winter unpleasantness by a late Florida departure. It wasn't what we had expected.

I remember when our beloved Aunt Alice was buried on April 21 in a rainy, turning to sleet, turning to thick snow Thursday in upstate New York. It was a miserable day. When we finally arrived at the cemetery and took the casket to the grave the heavens opened. A most gorgeous panorama of clouds and rays of golden sunshine lifted our heavy hearts to the heavens as we envisioned Aunt Alice resting with her parents and a baby brother who had died almost a century before. It wasn't what we expected!

I thought of my farmer father. Late snows meant it would be late spring before farmers could till the soil and prepare to plant the crops. Late springs mean that some crops were in danger of early autumn frosts, particularly the grapes in the Finger Lakes region, our home. My father had a more sanguine take on the situation. I laughed thinking about what my father always said that late spring snows were a poor man's fertilizer. Those snows helped turn the winter brown to spring green quickly.

Many times, life rolls out the unexpected. How did the angelomia get over here in the church garden? I planted it by the rose bushes. Why did the plumbago bloom white instead of blue at the time of Marilyn Ormiston's death? We often cannot fathom how things are working together. It is not what we expected. Peter Marty, editor of *Christian Century* was asking the same question of the "thorny" people in our lives in the April 24, 2018 issue. He suggested developing curiosity about other people and what gives them joy as a spiritual discipline to deal with those who oppose us, stand in our way, or are outright hostile. Curiosity, what gives joy, is a way to imagine how to move from "it's not what we had expected" to wonder how we might find common ground.

The Apostle Paul wrote about "it's not what we expected" in the Romans 8, NIV selected:

> "We know that all things work together for good for those who love God, who are called according to his purposes… If God is for us, who is against us? He who did not withhold his own Son, but gave him up for all of us, will he not with him also give us everything else? Who will bring any charge against us? … Who will separate us from the love of Christ? … For I am convinced that neither death, nor life, nor angels, or rulers, nor things present, nor things to come, nor height, nor depth, nor

> anything else in all creation, will be able to separate us from the love of God in Christ Jesus our Lord."

Pretty strong words for a fellow who persecuted Christians, was transformed through blindness, and then spent a good portion of his adult life being beaten, imprisoned, and on the lam. Probably not what he expected growing up a good and pious Jew, becoming a renowned Pharisee. Clearly Paul developed a curiosity about how God gives joy and devoted his life to it. Snow, and those things that are not what we expected, can become fertilizer for those who acknowledge their great need of God.

DEAR CHILDREN: A LETTER TO MY NIECES AND NEPHEWS

Dear Children,

I am a fan of letter writing. Psychologists tell us if we are struggling to communicate with a person, we are more likely to reach them if we respond to them in their preferred mode of communicating---a letter, an e-mail, a text, a phone call, or over coffee. I am not sure what your favorite mode is, but letters are so important to me that I thought I would try what works for me. But the idea of writing to "all my children—children, nieces and nephews" came from my niece Cindi who said she would like to sit down and talk with me. What a lovely compliment!

"These are times that try men's souls," was one of the typing exercises we would type in the dark ages when typing was taught in high schools. The events of the twenty-first century remind me that even though Thomas Paine wrote those words at the time of the American Revolution they capture the tenor of these days. We are suspicious, fearful, worried and we can't seem to move away from all the boiling pots in the American culture. They spill over into our personal lives and we have become more tentative in our relationships, afraid that we will further alienate someone who sits on the other side of some fence that has become a litmus test for our in-group. Or we become so angry at what we perceive to be the abdication of a core value that it doesn't matter who we strike out at verbally, we just can't live in this emotional pressure cooker without spouting off. It is a stressful, anxious way to live.

These times that try our souls certainly have revealed some of the worst of who we are as Americans. Much of our media is filled with the latest and greatest in virulent rhetoric and cruel caricature. The increased resorting to violence marks headlines, social media discussions, and indeed the number of our waking hours seemed to be filled with more of this fearful scenario.

Taking Your Own Temperature

I am trying to write a second book. I came home from Palestine in 2014 and knew the title would be "Better Than Right." This past fall I thought I'd better take a little reality check to make sure my issues weren't just getting projected on a larger screen. The Enneagram was my tool to look at myself and make sure I could write what's important without further adding to the pollution and noise of the present time. The Enneagram is an ancient spiritual tool to look at your life to discover which of the nine orientations your life has, and how it relates to the other eight postures. But the most astonishing notion for me was how this gift of your life also contained some huge negatives that explain how your life-themes and gifts contain dark sides that need to be redeemed to make life more pleasant, more connected, more joy-filled. Seeing that side of yourself in print and acknowledging, at least to yourself, that there is ample room to work on your own life issues brought my book-writing train to a siding. I was going to need to pause here, probably for far longer than I wanted to, to assimilate this new way of seeing myself and how I interact with my world. For the way I walk through the world has brought with it coping skills, but also brought distortions that make these trying times more difficult for me.

Let me illustrate. Part of who the Enneagram says I am, is a person who doesn't like to be on stage. I don't want too much exposure, for you're sure to see my faults and shortcomings. My gift is that people see me as a calm influence, a peacemaker. But part of my reluctance to be visible is that I can hold these beliefs and never have to do the hard work of tightening up arguments, stand for what I believe, so people could "have at" my ideas and challenge me to become clearer or change my viewpoint. I fear rejection and being discredited. I keep many beliefs and feelings hidden; but there is a cost involved and it takes a great deal of energy to keep this side of myself "under wraps." So what's to do in the meantime?

I have noted how public discourse has slipped into a thick morass that might make those who question the virtues of one's mother blush. A long-ago letter to the editor in the *Chicago Tribune* noted that whether "news" is true or not is of little importance these days. Is this really the end of the Age of Enlightenment, the flourishing of reason and empirical truths? How can we keep our fragile crafts afloat in such a turbulent sea, so full of flotsam?

So how do I start to be authentic and honor "your take" on the current hot topics? My dear husband proofreads what I write. He can sniff out where commas are needed; he can cut off my rambling sentences at the knees. But he would drive me crazy with his red pen and correctness. He got a green pen to remind me that there is growth in correction. Little help, I still fumed. A performance review goes better when the evaluator begins with the positive things. A reminder of connection and what that connection means in our lives we are not immediately put on the defensive in talking about tough things. We are aware of each other's humanity. ACE is learning if he can find one good thing to say about something I wrote first, the next part goes better.

I've come to believe, dear children, that it is in our saying the first good word that we, not the other person or people, are changed. It is our heart that has been opened to the possibility of seeing the connection, the goodness, the gift of the other first. Moving into an intense discussion now seems less confrontational. I am standing in some of our shared value. This value suggests that we may be able to look at our differences in a healing rather than a divisive light. In fact, before we ever get to the discussion we may be transported to a different perspective together without ever planning it. Sometimes standing in this light of our shared community, the line in the sand fades as winds blow where they will and we do not control them.

Pain and More Pain

At our small congregation in Florida we have community dinners once a month. One Saturday night I went to this dinner and ACE was out of town. A Vietnam veteran and I wound up at the table and he began talking about his military experience. I had never had the experience hearing a returning veteran's pain when he returned home after going off to war believing in what he had done and returning home to discover he was an object of scorn as many revelations about the conduct of the war came to light. An image emerged of a classically trained ballet dancer coming on stage to perform Swan Lake and when the lights come up and the music begins the dancer discovers it is a hip-hop show and tutus and slippers are out of place and sync. A howl goes up from the audience.

The veteran told me of his pain and rage when coming home, he was spit upon. The dance he trained to perform had changed. He was stunned that what he believed was his patriotic duty was now cast as inappropriate to the setting. Yet his life has been shaped by the Vietnam experience and his life has been limited by the Agent Orange that has damaged his lungs. His BFF is the portable oxygen pack that goes with him everywhere. He has been critically ill several times.

What I learned at our dinner was that the pain and hurt of one veteran who still bears the scars physically and emotionally from the Vietnam War is cut from the same cloth as my belief that war distorts us as people and as nations. Grown-ups, people and nations, have other ways to settle their differences. At that dinner table I heard of reshaping of one man's life and perspective because of that experience. It has softened me to the far-reaching effects of choices that we may not have been directly involved in and yet we still bear that burden. I am different, dear children, because I broke bread with a wounded warrior.

Other Choices

It would be easy to imagine how a spokesperson against apartheid in South Africa and leader of the Truth and Reconciliation Commission which tackled the difficult task of forgiveness, and another leader who was forced by the Chinese government to flee his kingdom and take his people into exile, would both be bitter over the cruelty and extermination of their people by cruel and powerful governments. It would be easy to imagine them loading their spiritual rifles to take aim at all the oppression, inhumanity, and injustice their people had endured. But through their long struggle they took time to be still. They have made other life-giving choices.

The Dalai Lama and Desmond Tutu celebrated the Dalai Lama's eightieth birthday at his home in exile in Dharamshala, India, a northern Indian state of Himachal Pradesh. The 100,000 Tibetan refugees who fled the Chinese invasion of Tibet appreciate the mountainous landscape and high altitude, reminding them of their homeland. The purpose of the Dalai Lama and Desmond Tutu's weeklong visit was a discussion of joy. Originally planned four years earlier, the Chinese government leaned on the South African government to deny the Dalai Lama a South African visa. But now the Tibetan holy man, in exile in India, and Tutu in poor health, gathered for a week and they talked of joy. There was much discussion of research into the states of the mind and body under various conditions for the Dalai Lama is a champion of science as it relates to various states in the human condition. In their long-awaited gathering there was laughter, touching of hands as the Dalai Lama often does as he greets and connects with people, and teasing. There was great respect as they talked about differences.

The Third Way

They planned their time together to talk about joy with the purpose of helping humanity unearth joy. These two men had experienced great suffering, personally and for their people and each man was a leader. The Dalai Lama was able to take a long view of his fifty years as a refugee. "It's more useful, more opportunities to learn, travel and experience life. There is a Tibetan saying: 'Wherever you have friends that's your country, and whenever you receive love, that's your home.'"[30]

When it was the Archbishop's time to reflect he recalled Nelson Mandela's twenty-seven years in Robbins Prison, many of those years in solitary confinement. Mandela went to jail, the angry, young head of the armed

---

[30] Dalai Lama, Desmond Tutu and Douglas Abrams *The Book of Joy* (NY: Random House, 2016) 56.

wing of the African National Congress. In those twenty-seven years of making big rocks into smaller rocks, he gained magnanimity and the dross burned off. Mandela came to see his enemies as human too, with hopes and expectations.[31] During those years Tutu was working on the outside, the voice of anti-apartheid resistance in South Africa. He received the Nobel Prize in 1984 for his work to end oppression of blacks and other persons of color.

How we face the suffering in our lives determines the outcome. Sometimes the pain is so intense we can only feel pain. But when we can unite our suffering with that of others, we reduce the intensity of our concentrated self-absorption. Obsessing about what you want and avoiding what you don't, doesn't lead to happiness. Buddhists believe that our natural state is joy. Sonja Lyubomirsky, a psychologist, studied suffering. She found that about half of it is determined by our genes and temperament, but the other half is a combination in which we do have some control, our attitudes and actions. She named how to work with the fifty per cent we can influence: reframe the situation positively, experience our gratitude, and choose to be generous.[32] That is a long menu to eat your way through when suffering arrives on your doorstep.

I think people who enter our lives with the radiance and joy of Archbishop Tutu and the Dalai Lama show us how to engage with the pain of our human experience. As they move into joy they pass through to forgiveness. Archbishop Tutu has written a book, *No Future Without Forgiveness* based on his work with the Truth and Reconciliation Commission in South Africa as the people tried to find a way forward through the atrocities of apartheid South Africa.[33]

---

[31] https://www.the.guardian.com/comment.is.free2013/dec/06/desmond-tutu-nelson-mandela.

[32] Sonja Travis Bradberry, "13 Things that Will Make You Happier," *Huff Post,* April 4, 2016, updated December 12, 2017.

[33] Desmond Tutu, *No Truth Without Forgiveness,* (NY: Doubleday, 1999).

The Mystery of Forgiveness

One of the mysteries of life is how easily, effortlessly really, we forgive sometimes. Things that are hurtful are blown away as a leaf or a feather. An incredible lightness returns to our spirit. Why sometimes, and not others? Why some people at sometimes and not others? *The Book of Joy* says we can develop this life of joy by the practices of quiet, prayer, discipline. Before you put this letter down in frustration at a bar raised so high you never could reach it, listen to Richard Rohr's three-step dance that may make the divide in our hearts a little easier to breach.

Rohr suggests that the first step is to choose the goodness in the other person over his/her faults. You know like the beginning of the Bible where God is busy creating everything and he says, "Hey, this is good." To those who have wronged you, failed to understand your perspective, or rudely dismissed you, simply say, "Hey, God made you. You are OK." Your starting point is just like God's. Seeing creation's purposes for goodness and joy.[34]

Secondly, we are to be open to the way that God's goodness flows through us. We can see ourselves in a new perspective as God's unique and precious child, designed to live in community with God and others.

The third step is not seeing the other as suddenly capitulating to your superior viewpoint, or wounded self. It has nothing to do with the other. Really. The third step is to experience your own capacity for goodness. It is a humbling thing to see that your choice can release some of the pain in the world, and within you. And you can go forward with fewer burdens strapped to your back. You can dance in the light of the first morning, you know, when God said, "It is good." It is good! It is also hard, but joy is the ineffable sign of the presence of God. Dear children, may we do the hard stuff so we can be helpers of each other's joy. With love to you all.

---

[34] Richard Rohr Daily Meditation, "The Natural World," March 10, 2018. Center for Action and Contemplation.

AS GOOD AS IT GETS

Texts: Psalm 84 and John 6:56-69

Things aren't like they used to be is a truism in our technological tennis match. Multiply that by a few decades and you can see some of the chasms of American culture. For example, in 1960 only five percent of American parents said they would be concerned if their son or daughter married someone from the opposition political party. Fifty years later, in 2010, 40 percent of the parents would be displeased if their children married across party lines. A lot has happened in fifty years. We have become fearful and contentious people. We complain we can't even get together with family for a barbecue or Thanksgiving anymore, because things blow up after the weather and football talk are exhausted.

Churches suffer from the same divisiveness. In the Civil Rights Era preachers set the national moral compass. They led marches, sat at segregated lunch counters until all people could be served there. They crossed bridges fortified with dogs to bring the promise of justice and equality to our country. Preachers tend to be much quieter these days. I confess that I am careful not to cross lines that would offend someone on the other side of the aisle for they just might leave the church and take a bunch of people with them. Better to check the ice to be sure the ice isn't thin. The 21st century church is accused of being irrelevant and out of touch, or worse, mirroring the worst fears instead of the brightest hopes of our life together.

Foreign Policy magazine surveyed national security experts recently and asked what was the likelihood that the United States would enter an armed civil war. The experts put the probability at 30 percent.[35] The rifts are deep. Human suffering abounds. Before even starting to speak, detractors will tell the church to check its own house first. They will point to decades of sexual abuse, particularly of children. Millions of dollars have been paid in damages in these cases. But it is more encompassing than that. The church bears responsibility to care for those the least of these, to protect the vulnerable and to be a moral exemplar. To get there the church needs to enter in that right relationship with God. That is no small task. But doing that painful work, eating the Bread of Life that Jesus was talking about might be as good as it gets! It certainly didn't have great appeal in the Capernaum synagogue where Jesus was teaching that morning.

Speaking of Losses

Our Judeo-Christian history is littered with losses. One of the most painful for the Jews was the loss of the temple at the time of the Babylonian exile, about 2,500 years ago. After the Jews longed for a king, King David brought the ark to Jerusalem, and it was David's son, Solomon, who finally built the temple! In the words of HGTV, it was to be "their forever home!" Every year people went up to Jerusalem to celebrate God's delivering the Jews from slavery in Egypt. Every year the foot-sore pilgrims climbed and sang, remembering their roots, recalling their forebears, and most of all, thanking God for this lovely dwelling place. They could see the temple in their mind's eye. This trip only increased their devotion and joy. They were going to Zion, the holy temple in the holy city! It was as good as it gets!

But the temple fell in 586 BCE when the Babylonians conquered Judah and demolished the temple. You can imagine the pain as the Jews walked from Judah into exile! The tangible aspects of their faith and the pinnacle, the temple, destroyed. Tears and anger must have flowed on that long walk.

It doesn't take much to imagine the travail of those who today walk through the Mexican desert to escape gang wars, drugs and violence, or

---

[35] https://faithandleadership.com/allen-r-hinton-country-polarized-how-can-christian-help

Ethiopians in leaky boats on the Mediterranean Sea being refused port, or prisoners in Cook County Jail awaiting trials, some waiting for ten years without a trial. There are some days when it is difficult to sing about God's lovely dwelling place.

Jesus' disciples were no different than most of us. They loved the temple but they were following Jesus. They loved the wonder, drama and excitement of feeding the 5,000, the jaw-dropping spectacle of Jesus walking on the water to catch up with their boat in stormy seas. This was heady stuff!

The very next day, when the racing heart rates returned to normal, Jesus began digging into the course syllabus. This is more difficult than conquering the pounding waves. Jesus confronts his disciples: you were looking for me this morning because the mighty signs of God grabbed your attention. You wanted to be sure you signed up for the power, a few loaves of bread that can feed 5,000 and feet that can conquer even the tempestuous storm. Ah, I have something more difficult for you to chew on. I want to give you bread that will satisfy forever.

The disciples leaned forward. Feeding 5,000, walking on water, and now bread forever. This was better than they expected, even from Jesus. "What do we have to do?"

"Throw your lot in with the One whom God has sent. That kind of commitment gets you in on God's works," Jesus said. Those who had seen the feeding of the 5,000 and Jesus walking on water were clueless. "Give us a sign, just one more," they pleaded. I wonder about the look that must have crossed Jesus' face as the disciples asked for some more.

Our history is the story of the long haul as people of God. But before we portray Jesus' disciples as utterly hopeless category, let's look at Psalm 84: How lovely is God's dwelling place, where even sparrows find a home, where parched souls find cool springs. Who wouldn't want to serve as gatekeeper for their God in that temple? The disciples are caught in a paradox: they are serving God by fulfilling the rules for living as a faithful Jew worshipping in the temple. But what were they to do with the disquiet of the oppressed in a conquered territory in the first century Roman

Empire? They must have been impressed when Herod's grandiose second temple was built. It had become lovelier and lovelier. God's lovely dwelling place is as good as it gets!

If You Don't Stand for Something, You'll Fall for Anything

But the people come to Jesus and Jesus distributes the syllabus for the disciples: Believe in the One whom God has sent, get on board for this dwelling place of God. Your understanding of faith will have to grow into God's vision. It's that simple. Believing in the One whom God has sent will ramp up your understanding of how to live as God's people. You will gladly swap bread for 5,000 for the bread of eternal life. But it was not an easy concept for them to grasp.

Jesus asked a huge leap of faith from his followers: an attitude adjustment time. I am the One who will show you now how God wants to you live, Jesus begins. It isn't the temple as centerpiece of faith. Stress fractures between the Jewish leaders and Jesus begin to show. The disciples grumble. "This is difficult. Who can accept this?" they groan.

Throughout history there are some who understood that the church would always be on the move. One hymn laments, "New occasions teach new duties/Time makes ancient good uncouth/They must upward still and onward/ Who would keep abreast of truth." Like the country and Western folk singer, Willy Nelson, they just couldn't wait to get on the road again to see where the giver of this eternal bread would be lead. For those who get Jesus, body and soul, it changes them. It's a long road from slavery in Egypt to building the temple and an even more treacherous journey to Jesus' command to eat his body and live in God's lovely dwelling place. But to those who would call the road Jesus trod home it was as good as it gets.

Rev. Dr. William Barber II is the architect of the new Poor People's Campaign. The first one was begun by Dr. Martin Luther King 50 years ago. Rev. Barber organizes marches around the country to increase awareness of the tremendous cost of injustices of systemic racism and poverty today. He was in Chicago in Summer 2018 to raise awareness of the tremendous cost of gun violence there. His followers marched from the South Side to Lake Shore Drive via the Kennedy Expressway to call attention to the loss of life and fabric of society by business-as usual-attitude within the city, and within government.

He regularly receives death threats against himself, his wife and their five children. Rev. Barber has every reason to lament and be defeated. He suffers from a debilitating form of arthritis, but he crisscrosses the country with his call for action against injustice. The pastor admits to becoming pessimistic at times. But he tries to remain hopeful because he's required to be hopeful. "There comes a time when you gotta stop mourning and pick yourself up," the pastor says. And if somebody ever tells him again that this is the worst we've ever seen in America he really gets excited! "You tired, and folk had to fight: 200 years against slavery and 150 years against Jim Crow? You tired, and women had to fight for the vote? We got the nerve to talk about tired? I'm tired of what I see happening, and I'm rested, and ready to fight," says the tireless civil rights champion.[36]

Rev. Barber's vision of the church sharply contrasts with those that moan about the good old days. The charge of irrelevance of the church needs to encounter that spirit of Rev. Barber who abides in the body of Jesus and has eternal life flowing through his arthritic body. To be on the road with Jesus is as good as it gets.

Yet we know today churches become attached to "their church." There are many congregations that are saddled with old buildings and dwindling membership who can't envision another life apart from their church real estate. To their minds, there is no other way to be church. They would be right there with those who didn't get what Jesus was talking about, the church as bread of life versus those who knew what street corner to find their church. Bread of Lifers know church is more than an address.

In John 6: 68-69 Peter understands what Jesus offered in this bread. "To whom would we go? You have the words of real life, eternal life. We've

[36] https://www.motherjones.com/politics2018/07/im-rested-and-ready-to-fight-the-reverend-barbers-battle-cry-is-one-for-the-ages

already committed ourselves, confident that you are this Holy One of God." Jesus' offer of bread did not come with the temple attached. To be in God's dwelling place was going to be where common, ordinary, brown, frequently chirping too loudly sparrows would be welcome. To be in God's dwelling place would be where thirsty Palestinians would not have their water supply shut off indefinitely by the Israeli government; where the residents in Flint, Michigan and Chicago Heights, Illinois could turn on their tap water and know it was free of deadly contaminants. Somehow Psalm 84 had morphed into the notion of a glorious temple, much like we envision the beautiful edifice of our church with manicured lawns, and healthy families strolling in the sunlight to worship. Herod had enlarged and augmented the temple, bigger and better; it played well with the people. The psalm had become paean to that structure that Ezra and Nehemiah envisioned as the center of Judah's worshipping community amid the frequent takeovers by foreign powers. And Jesus, the good docent that he is, points out how a religious idea had become a religious institution whose use and function had veered sharply from its mission statement.

Jesus offers us the alternative: The Bread of Life which, when eaten, sustains and transforms the followers into those who have eternal life. And that is as good as it gets. But to get there the notion of what it means to be a church must undergo rigorous scrutiny. A church with a history or a church with a future? A building or a way of life? An institution with founding principles or living stones with God's purposes in mind on the journey? On the road again, and being there is as good as it gets.

Let's review. The Hebrew children were on the road out of Egypt to a place promised by God. It was as good as it gets. The Israelites brought the ark of the covenant into the Promised Land and built a temple to honor God. On the road again. It was as good as it gets. Jesus, the Son of Man, as usual, is on the road. He commands us to strengthen ourselves so we too can do the work God has for us. It is as good as it gets. And many like Pastor Barber remind us that being on the road is a long haul, but it is as good as it gets. Amen.

NORTHERN GARDENER

Pruning

Back in Florida the warm winter sun feels good after the snowstorm that marked our departure from Illinois! Everything has been growing since we left seven months ago, among them, our trees and shrubs. Action is needed. We called the same man who trimmed the trees in the church garden last spring. Our flowering maple had grown so big no grass grew on our neighbor's front yard. It had blocked out the sun. The pink powder puff was full of the loveliest, soft blossoms twenty feet up, well hidden by the undergrowth that didn't blossom. The canopy of three oak trees had become overly dense, a ready target for a stray hurricane's hungry dance. A garden, like life, is a process.

Last Saturday a truck, four men and a chipper arrived. For the better part of the day, they sawed, dragged heavy branches, and the chipper ground endlessly. Their last act was to dig up a papaya tree that had sprung up uninvited at the front of the house. It wasn't there when we left and in seven months it was over twelve feet tall and had several papayas growing on it. The men carefully dug it up and were going to try to transplant it to their garden.

When they left, our house looked different. There were some spindly trunks of flowering maple and powderpuff with a few wisps of scrawny branches offering no shade for our patio. The oak trees had been transformed into stately *grande dames* anchoring our lawn. The arborist, like a good barber, found the cut that enhanced the subject and revealed its natural beauty.

I imagined a conversation among the trees when they saw the truck pull up:

> **Powder puff**: Here comes trouble.
> **Flowering maple**: It is going to hurt.
> **Oak tree**: I don't know about you but I feel like I need to get rid of some of my top. It's just too heavy. I am going to be a whole new tree!

Pruning and shaping is always a gamble. Too severe pruning and the tree dies. Improper pruning equates to butchery. There could be a drought that would throw the tree into shock and it would die. We just don't know when the pruning takes place what the result will be ---more fruit or a devastating loss.

Jesus talked about when our lives get pruned. When our lives are cut and shaped we may be like the maple and know it's really going to hurt. We dread how what we think are our loveliest parts will be stripped from us. It's going to be painful. At the least, we are like the powder puff tree and know trouble and upheaval are coming. But Jesus had another viewpoint on pruning. Jesus saw it as those who are rooted in God being shaped to bear more fruit in the community. God was the root, and the community in Christ would be shaped by God's design, to grow more fruit. Shaping in God creates a beauty not measured by the world's exacting standards but by God who creates us for community, not for an individualistic relationship with God, but for community with relationships and responsibilities to and for each other and with God.

The trees are trimmed. We must watch and see how the trees respond to their shaping. When our lives are pruned, we have relationships and responsibilities to God and to each other. We are part of the vine, which is our sustenance. We need to rely on the community of Christ and lean into the new persons we are shaped into being by the arborist with the plans, wonderful plans. Let's being vigilant to see how we, as a community, are being shaped to bear much fruit.

SPREAD YOUR WIDE WINGS

Born to us a tiny baby
Born today to life anew
Water touches your sweet forehead
Holy Spirit, gift from you.
Sacrament, strengthen believers
Faith, ground us, make us true
Now as in all time God's promises
Reveal Christ, Creator, you.

Little children, be our leaders
Childlike trust proves good and fair.
Where despair, defeat and anger
Child laughter clears the air.
Sweep away dense, foggy notions
Of worlds we can create.
Laughing, playing and rejoicing
Child of God we celebrate.

Spread your wings wide and explore God's world
Earth is waiting for your touch.
Kittens, puppies, kids and old ones
Each life means oh so much.
Child of God, claimed in the spirit

Child, giv'n to servanthood
Rooted, may you soar to wonder
Child, spread your unique good.

Celebrating the birth of our first grandchild on January 10, 1999.
Hymn Tune: Swedish folk tune *Breda Dina Vida Vingar*

GEORGE'S FAMILY

We gathered in an ordinary hotel meeting room on the mezzanine looking out on an enclosed balcony. It was 9 a.m. day one in Beijing. There were thirty-one of us at the time, four we were told, had had flight delays and would arrive later that day. Our tour guide climbed up on a bar stool with a small podium in front of him and began to speak. He wore a red windbreaker and T-shirt and grey travel pants, the kind that are easily washed in a hotel sink and are dry the next morning.

He began: For the next twenty days we would have a new identity. We would be "George's family." We would now become a part of his family, George Zhangke, Chengdu, China. He would be our country guide as we trekked, most of us for the first time, from Beijing to Shanghai, to Chongquin to Xian to Guilin to finally to be swooshed through the birth canal of this burgeoning, ancient culture, Hong Kong. He would host, provide entrance and explanation for all the new wonders and challenges we would experience in this culture foreign to our experience, a history that makes our two-century existence as a country look like nursery school.

He would teach us diplomacy, grace, self- control and responsibility and how to deal with stressful and new situations. He simply took us in as we were and made us his. George began by giving us a "velvet" lecture, laced with humor and grace on the importance being punctual, prepared and ready for the next adventure. The first twenty minutes, essentially of the first-day-of-school lecture, of how we were his family. His speech was peppered with "George's family" as each of us had embedded in our psyches the exact inflection of his voice as he announced it over and over again, "George's family" and we knew the next words out of his mouth were going to be important: directions on how to proceed and navigate China's culture and customs, or an important piece of China's story. But he didn't mention that, after twenty-one days with him, we would be able to see ourselves in a new light.

In my childhood I had the red lettered edition of the Bible where every word Jesus spoke was written in red letters. Those red letters were important words. In John Irving's book, *A Prayer for Owen Meany*, Owen had this squeaky, high-pitched voice throughout his life and Irving put everything Owen said in capital letters and soon I had internalized Owen's voice in my head. Here in China our group would all "listen up" when our guide said, "George's family" for he would began a snippet of his own living through the Cultural Revolution with his father and mother whom he called "two tigers living on the same mountain." He also told how his parents and his grandparents experienced China's Cultural Revolution and the Red Guard. I came to treasure his experiences which gave the true flavor of his motherland. Trusting that when our two hearts stood up together straight and tall we would not only see that China but also our own motherland, as faulted and flawed, but also complex and offering each us, by virtue of birth, a chance to live far beyond our self-defined scope or intent. He modeled a larger identity.

George has a three-year-old son whose Chinese name means Little Potato. He and his wife chose that name because they want their son to be grounded in his ordinariness, not in his exceptionality. But Little Potato does have a distinct advantage. His father was a consummate teacher. He taught didactically, pedagogically, patiently and gracefully. He gave us careful preparation---exactly what it would be like to go through airport security on the five intra-Chinese flights. He broke it down into easily assimilated learning like the five elements of airport check-in luggage security. He thoroughly prepared us for each day's adventure---what we would be experiencing and the significance of each encounter. And then, as a wise teacher, he let us experience it. Afterwards, he received our comments, and did not deflect our reactions, even negative ones.

Even our mealtimes were teaching moments as he explained each item the busy waitresses and waiters ferried to the lazy susan. He personally brought vegetarian and gluten-free items to those with special dietary restrictions and choices. He explained the drink policy of each restaurant which usually was one free drink for each meal. It could be Coke, Sprite, beer or bottled water. It only took one encounter with Chinese wine, which was an up-charge, to figure out there were better choices in China. There was little grousing, a frequent American syndrome, as the restaurants the tour company had selected were varied in the type of Chinese cuisine they offered and the palatably-homesick were offered two dinners where we ordered from an anglicized menu. We ate seaside in the New Territories, in a harbor filled with yachts and big boats. We walked to the restaurant past tanks filled with cuttlefish, giant clams, prawns which frequently made jailbreak only to arrive on the slippery floor below, and a bevy of crabs sporting variously-colored and striped shells. We dined in restaurants featuring Chinese dumplings, Chinese noodles, food presented in artistic arrangement and restaurant-theatre venues. We ate fried rice three meals a day as it was always included in the breakfast buffet. We knew our dining experience was close to the finale of the meal when a platter of watermelon wedges arrived. Watermelon was on the breakfast buffets also.

The freshest fish-to-market delivery we saw was cruising on the Li River in Guilin when fishermen on boats made of PVC pipe and small motors would pull alongside the cruise boats and present their catch in netted poles to the cooks who were preparing the meals for the passengers. George's family had boxed lunches from shore that day. We trekked through markets with ducks and chickens awaiting the hatchet, eggs of every description, and a plethora of Chinese fruits, vegetables and herbs.

George taught us gracefully. A foreign country is a feast for the mind and heart and often chaos for the stomach. When travelers encountered that phenomenon George would pick up the bus microphone and ask, "Do you have a time for a joke?" and our smiling host, who could laugh at himself so freely, would diffuse any impatience with his story-telling prowess.

One sacred time for me was the Sunday afternoon as we cruised the Yangtze from Yichang to Chongquin. George reserved a large meeting room on our ship and invited anyone who would like to meet his "other family." For an hour and a half, George shared tiny photos, carefully sealed in small Ziploc bags that held the recorded treasures of his forty-one years as the only child of a mechanical engineer and a doctor, who were forced to live in the countryside during the revolution and then come back from the country to earn $8 a month as an engineer and $7 a month as a doctor. George described his father as a genius, a protégé of a PhD in mechanical engineering. His father had designed lock lifts on the Three Gorges Dam. But George is his father's son. He is a genius of the human condition. For the younger Zhangke taught by example, by being thoroughly prepared, by knowing how the system works, by doing the amazing difficult task of getting all the plates spinning at the same time and making it look simple. He taught through the strength of his character. He did not complain. He told us how we were now part of "George's family." His family of origin had experienced starvation, deprivation in a community that included those who lived in their "hutong" where 15 or 20 families shared life, joys, sorrows, victories and losses and a 7-inch black and white TV which his family saved and scrimped for and then brought out into a courtyard on a snake of extension cords so everyone in the community could enjoy it. They also shared one communal bathroom for everyone in their "hutong." George's father, mother and George lived in that one-room apartment which they shared with another family from 1979 to 2000. That experience and his parents' teachings profoundly shaped him.

One of the few colored pictures George showed us that Sunday gathering was of him and his wife when they had saved up enough money to go to the photographer a few years after they were married. It was, George confessed, the only time in his life that he had worn a suit, and it was a rented suit, for the photograph. George described himself as a "soft-eared husband" that meant as his wife "chewed on his ear" with things she would like, he became amenable to her desires over time and through a careful savings plan they would buy. Amazingly he could work with us and not dwell on the hugely-different standard of living we represented. Instead he brought the well-honed capacity to understand each carries a precious seed of humanity regardless of circumstances.

There was part of George's family we never were formally introduced to but we met them everywhere. These were "my cousins," as George called them. George's cousins took our bags from the airports to the hotel. George's cousins were shopkeepers, sanitation workers in public restrooms, airport security personnel, waiters and waitresses and George explained how we should treat them and a few words to greet them respectfully. Referencing them as cousins kept Americans laughing at the various mores needed to manage a culture quite diverse, yet in many ways, remarkably similar to our own. George would explain how and when to bargain and when it was impossible or not acceptable. Our own speech was soon sprinkled with references to George's cousins when we encountered aggressive shopkeepers or street sellers or in a government-owned shop.

George taught us how to be good tourists. Through the morass of those arrangements and special requests George was able to focus and shepherd us through twenty-one days of eye-opening, heart-rending complexity that is China. At the farewell banquet, George received a standing ovation from the group. Over and over I heard people remark what a congenial group we were. I looked over at George laughing and smiling with us and I thought George must be laughing on the inside too, for he had taught us so well we thought we had done it ourselves. For three weeks we had been "George's family." Here we had discovered our best selves--- alive and well and visiting China.

THE NORTHERN GARDENER GOES TO CHINA

Visiting a formal Chinese garden built with a house surrounding it on four sides gave me new insights about how to live together on this crowded planet. At the center of this garden was *not* a huge pond that could be viewed from any window that would essentially offer the same view. Rather, each window opening into the courtyard offered a different landscape. Each window revealed another vista. Each window into a Chinese garden is a new scene whether a tree, rocks, or a couple of bushes, or koi swimming in the water is the focus.

Perhaps at the next window you notice the back of some tall rocks and two skinny pine trees pointing to heaven. Walking along an outside of this garden you might see a beached boat artistically placed at the shore and the graceful pale-flowered frangipani tree overhead at the next window. Here stones create a path to the shore through a lush ground cover of tiny plants. Each scene within the garden is unique and beautiful.

Last January I heard Barbara Brown Taylor speak at a Gladdening Light conference in Winter Park, Florida. She talked about her book, *Holy Envy*. The phrase "holy envy" comes from Martin Buber, a Jewish scholar. It means to look at another--- religion, property, person, or even a country--- and see them as having some good qualities we very much like. It does not mean we have to have them or possess them for ourselves. Rather there are good qualities, part of their creation in God's vast creation, which are attractive to us. Taylor's book expounds on finding qualities in others which opens us up to true appreciation and joy without having to make them our own. Walking through that rather small garden showed me how those gardeners envisioned offering so many views, each unique. Each to be appreciated and enjoyed.

Seeing this garden in China reminded me of the huge chasm between the US and China and yet "different gardens" in China depended upon which window you were looking from. To appreciate the view is to see beauty anywhere as a gift from God, whether in China or in the church garden. Gardens are for developing our eyes to the magic and mystery of God's beautiful world. To do that we need clean windows. Our windows sometimes get clouded with cynicism, despair, and isolation, not at all ready to take in all the beauty God has planned for us. Gardens are for restoring our sight and our souls.

PECKING ORDER

Roger Tory Peterson's 1934 classic, *A Field Guide to the Birds,* puts pigeons and doves in the same family: *columbidae.* The rock dove, or domestic pigeon, *columba livia*, hardly gets a sterling introduction. Peterson says, "This bird has become feral in places and is as firmly established as a wild species as the house sparrow or starling. It needs no introduction."[37]

The *columba livia* is at the very bottom of Peterson's *columbidae* pecking order. But in my mind, it is a long walk from the pigeons overtaking the underpasses on the El in Chicago to the white dove sleeping on the sand, of Peter, Paul and Mary's glory days. But even within the *columbidae* family there is a pecking order and the domestic pigeon, seldom called by its dove name, is at the bottom of the heap.

Yet my husband and I love to sit on our patio and watch the birds. From there we concur with the Audubon assessment that one in four birds has disappeared in the last half century in North America. That is nearly three billion fewer birds.[38] There have been no hummingbirds sighted around our house or a favorite haunt on Linear Park. The palm warbler, once a flashy garden visitor with his flitting tail and Johnny One Note song, made a few cameo appearances in December and was gone. Jesus' words in Matthew 25:40 NSRV, … "Truly I tell you, just as you did it to one of the least of these who are members of my family, you did it to me" are truly meant

---

[37] Roger Tory Peterson, *A Field Guide to the Birds* (Boston and NY: Houghton Mifflin, 1934) 84.

[38] "New Study finds U.S. and Canada have lost more than 1 in 4 birds in the past 50 years" Division of Environmental Biology<https://www.nsf.gov/awardsearch/showAward?AWD_ID=1661259&HistoricalAwards=false>

for our fellow inhabitants who are being pushed to extinction by a ruthless pecking order.

Understanding Social Location

Our patio bird list now includes the mockingbirds, who still love to sing and engage in their strange flitting and menacing courtship routines, the blackbirds, crows and starlings, turkey vultures circling on thermals high overhead and a few mourning doves. Two mourning doves have claimed our neighbor's backyard and shrubs and they are there all day. We were quite excited to see one morning a white-winged dove pacing on our glass-topped patio table looking in the window at us. For three mornings she came and checked in on us, cocking her head from side to side to make sure she was seeing us correctly. I guess we passed the test for she has never come back. Places to go, people to see… We laughed, my husband and I. We would have never thought we would be looking forward with so much enthusiasm to seeing a member of the pigeon family check in on us.

We, like our bird friends, are moving down the pecking order as we are well past retirement age. We notice that we don't drive as well as we used to, we need more candle power to read the fine print. We forget words, and certainly we are slowing down, and although we try to keep up, our grandchildren find us old-fashioned. We wish others would defer to our judgment based on all our years of experience and yet we bristle when people treat us as helpless and useless. Technology has added another foreign language which makes us run to catch up and try to learn the language that our grandchildren have known since they first held those tiny hand-held devices in their chubby toddler hands. Acknowledging our diminishment, living into it with grace and humor, is a task that requires a lot of pondering as each life rung brings new status, and like it or not, aging moves us down the pecking order.

Not in My Block

Wendell Berry's book, *Unsettling America* notes that the underlying assumptions about the land and agriculture have become so pervasive that we never stop to question them.[39] They are normative, describing our reality. Today experts, particularly agriculture professors, corporate experts, engineers, and numbers crunchers, tell us what will work and what the future will hold. Using their models, they point to the glorious future--- efficient, extremely productive, and free from drudgery. Farms will use only five percent of the population to grow food for the nation, and not only that, they will be so efficient that they can grow food for a hungry world. Fields will be gigantic, animals located on huge feed lots and the corporate farmer will live in areas devoted to recreation and leisure.

This nirvana, championed by then-Secretary of Agriculture Earl Butz in Eisenhower and Nixon's administrations, is agribusiness. Agribusiness moved the small farmer far down the pecking order from producer of the food for America's tables to problem status. Small farmers migrated from the farm into the city where they become someone's else's problem, the chink in someone else's model: unskilled labor in the cities. Berry elegantly exposes how the American notion of technological superiority has created a waste product: people who cannot produce as much food as behemoth farm equipment nor who have the need for millions of tons of fertilizers to squeeze more pounds of food out of the soil because the animal and plant wastes are no longer nearby or utilized in revitalizing the soil. Their small equipment and perhaps their farm animals did not create the need for fuel to deplete reserves and endanger air and water quality. Their crop rotation, contour farming, lying fallow, and crop diversity were sound practices that did not become technological problems for the Corps of Engineers and agricultural experts to solve as farms became bigger. The small farmers' equipment did not compact the soil, nor destroy the homes of some of the "least of these" who inhabited hedgerows and swamps. More diversity meant less soil erosion.

---

[39] Wendell Berry, *Unsettling America* (Berkeley: Counterpoint, 1977) 51.

Economy of Scale

Hunger was a global problem after World War II. How could this problem be solved most efficiently? The United States clearly was a vast canvas with resources, ingenuity, and compassion to tackle it. We had the reputation for problem solving. With single-minded purpose, a new vision shaped our land. We were, after all, steeped in enlightenment methodology and our prowess had been proven in the factories, laboratories, and battlefields of World War II. A new war, this time on hunger was just the challenge technology needed. The bloom of success flushed our cheeks and offered direction to our marshalled energies. We would feed the hungry masses from our wide prairies and fertile farmlands.

But the fallacy of these models and organizational blueprints stumbles in exactly the place that mystics have wrestled with the dominant culture and headed to the wilderness. Who's in and who's out? How are the decisions reached and who makes them?

The solutions to the agricultural dilemma depend on who gets to offer solutions and to swim to the head of the class with the "right" answer. Today's swimming pool is for volume and efficiency. The solution to intransigent problems is circumscribed by how the problem is defined. There is a world of perceptual difference between a pigeon or rock dove. Simply by moving the small farmer off the land onto the urban planners' desks was a lateral transfer in the pecking order. The greater good debate, while acknowledging today's complexity, seems to settle on what's good for those who are defining the problem, their technology and vision to see world beyond.

For instance, how can you not thank the Bill and Melinda Gates Foundation with its motto, "All lives have equal value?" Microsoft has forever changed our world. Their worth is $111.3 billion dollars according to Forbes. They use their enormous profits to make the world a healthier place. Their dollars back up initiatives. But there have been costs measured in quality of life for their largess. A wide-angle lens sees the playing field on a planet that needs energy and capital to continue those lucrative practices. An article in the *Los Angeles Times* in January 2007 illustrates how the generosity of the Gates Foundation has a shadow side hidden from the camera's view at the press conferences announcing huge grants for noble endeavors like measles vaccinations and immunizations for polio for children. For example, as the Foundation spent $218 million on measles and polio immunizations worldwide.[40]

Children in the Niger Delta received those immunizations but the Gates Foundation did not help "the cough" which is how Nigerians describe the asthma, bronchitis and blurred vision of children in this area as they live where flames spew 300 feet into the air from the oil plants run by Eni, Royal Dutch Shell, Exxon Mobil, Chevron and Total of France blanketing Ebocha, Nigeria with their toxicity. It is cheaper for those companies to burn one billion cubic feet of gas than to sell it. The Gates Foundation has invested $423 million in those companies. They, in turn, reap vast financial gains from investments that contravene their health initiatives.

A New Earth

We are plopped down in our moment in history, cusp between old and new: end of the enlightenment and the crowning of human reason, and the dawn of the digital age, and artificial intelligence. A dilemma ensues: is it a race or paralysis? Do we rush into the fray with solutions, grabbing our technological toolkit, or do we stand back, watch, gather information, trying to get a sense of the context? We can't possibly have all the information needed to make a wise decision. Now the models theory of problem solving confronts the astrophysicists' assertions that we are living in an expanding universe. So much for a geocentric or heliocentric universe. Welcome to the cosmic universe where we open ourselves up to the possibility of mystery and awe that far transcends our human models. Some crises demand immediate answers. But being thoughtful, Berry argues, means slowing down, where we may lose our place in line,

---

40 Charles Piller et al., "Dark Clouds Over Good Works of the Gates Foundation" *Los Angeles Times,* January 7, 2007.
https://www.latimes.com/archives/la-xpm-jan-07-na-gatesx07-storyhtml

falling lower in the pecking order to gain wisdom and clarity about the way forward. The celebration of our gifts has within it the seeds of our destruction. Nothing new here. But is that all?

Beyond Dualism

Throughout history, there has been a remnant who turned away from the dominant culture to find a wholistic answer that doesn't deny or exclude any part of the birth, growth, maturity, death, and decay cycle. It includes pigeons, old people, small farmers and children who live in the Nigerian delta. While our culture tends to focus on the birth, growth, maturity of the cycle, the wise have noticed that death and decay are needed for life to go forward.

Placed on the downward side of this cycle is pecking order mentality. My husband and I are neither the producers nor consumers we used to be. Our value in the marketplace has diminished. We buy fewer big-ticket items. We are trying to downsize only to find the next generation isn't interested in our treasures or those for whom we were stewards from previous generations. Our social location like the rest of humanity, is moving.

Wendell Berry talks about how the models in agricultural science have moved us farther from locating ourselves in history. This Kentucky philosopher sees the small farmer becoming superfluous, an outsider, and a waste in problem-solving models. Concentrating farmland into larger holdings with fewer farmers moves the focus to consequences of overhead, debt, technology, and the capacity of machines to become financially accountable and defeat the competition. Agriculture, the unifying cycle that preserves health, fertility and renewal in nature, has been sliced and diced into models that include ways to prosper, where bigger is better, and incidentally makes use of their favored technology which incidentally becomes profitable and promotes the ideal of the model makers' tightly controlled and circumscribed parameters. Missing is the mysterious, complex, and playful interdependence where human culture joins the natural world. We have become embedded in the orthodoxy of agriculture.[41]

He would agree with Irish priest/poet John O'Donohue who wrote,

> "You have traveled too fast over false ground
>
> Now your soul has come to take you back."[42]

The Little Pieces in the Big Picture

Here's where it starts to get interesting! Theologian Paul Tillich described God as the Ground of Being. Berry comes along and breathes life into that very ground, much as Genesis 2:7 did. He looks at the soil as the matrix of culture and community. He sees the distinctions between body and soul, health and dis-ease, heaven and earth as false dichotomies limiting the infinite and expanding universe. The fallout of the pecking order is exclusion of missing parts of the healthy whole. Ecclesiastes 3:1 NRSV notes, "For everything there is a season and a time for every matter under heaven." Nothing excluded.

The wildness, wilderness, and what some deem as waste, have much to teach us about healthy living on the farm. Sir Albert Howard wrote to learn to preserve the farm, we must study the forest.[43] Just as body and spirit, individuals and community are susceptible to influence they are also conductors of each other's realities. It is as the environmentalists tell us we cannot just do one thing. To include, not dominate or overcome, to heal, complicates things. To use Martin Buber's "I-Thou" notion of encounter is the honoring of the sacredness of each other's experience and context. Health comes in the process and the cycle of birth, growth, maturity, death

---

[41] Berry, 178.

[42] John O'Donohue, *Aram Cara: A Book of Celtic Wisdom* (NY: Harper Collins, 1997) 227-229.

[43] Sir Albert Howard, *The Soil and Health,* (NY: Schocken Paperback edition, 1972) 78. Quoted in Berry, 146.

and decay are in balance. The most foundational health is the ground beneath our feet.

Dandelions in the Sidewalks

Healing the earth is in concert with healing our own brokenness, within ourselves, within our relationships, within and between communities and our Mother Earth herself. Pecking orders are competitive markers necessary to affirm the rightness of our position. Finding ourselves, our roles, appreciating the variety and complexity of a whole earth is broken open anew each day.

Look at Jacob's experience as he ran from his brother Esau (Gen 28:16-17 NRSV). Jacob was on the lam because he had cheated his brother out of his birthright. Esau had sworn vengeance. While Jacob is fleeing, he slept in the desert with his head on a stone. He dreamed there was a ladder between heaven and earth and angels ascending and descending it. God told Jacob that the land on which he is sleeping God would give to him and his descendants, and they will become as dust, covering the earth. God will keep faith with him. Suddenly Jacob awoke and cried, "Surely the presence of the Lord in is this place,--- and I didn't even know it. How awesome is this place! This is none other than the house of God, and this is the gate of heaven." Recognizing our place and the holy ground beneath our feet, opens to the world that has been there all along, the world of wholeness and health. After revealing the beauty of what has been here all along, Berry's poem, "What We Need Is Here" concludes:

> ...And we pray, not
> for new earth or heaven, but to be
> quiet in heart, and in eye,
> clear, What we need is here.[44]

---

[44] Wendell Berry, "The Wild Geese" *Selected Poems* (Berkeley: Counterpoint, 1998) 90.

NORTHERN GARDENER

Stones in Your Shoes, Rocks in Your Garden

Back in Illinois I am nearing the end of spring cleaning, planting, and mulching in our garden. Last winter was really cold which makes spring extra beautiful because the bulbs have had a long winter's nap. Daffodils were blooming by the fence when we arrived home. Tulips and grape hyacinths were budded out front. Add the extravagant beauty of the flowering quince and hostas peeping their pointed heads through the ground. Yes, there was work that had to be done. Leaves had to be pulled away from the beds they'd been covering all winter. Dandelions cried for my husband's attention. He patrols our lawn and the neighbor's sometimes twice a day to eradicate any yellow heads and jagged leaves emerging with thoughts of procreation.

But today is for another insight in my gardening schema. Most annoying to me is to be hard at work and suddenly find a pebble has surreptitiously jumped into my shoe and this tiny two millimeter demon, remnant of a prehistoric disturbance, can suddenly wedge between foot and shoe and demand to be dealt with. Each step reminds me who is in charge. I try to ignore it as long as possible hoping it will slip to a place where foot and stone can coexist within my shoe. Pebbles always win. I have to stop, lean against something, untie my shoe, remove the sock and evict the culprit. I wonder if the tiny hitchhiker laughs as it tumbles to the ground looking forward to the next time when it can shout, "Gotcha!" But it does make a very valid point: it is often the tiniest of things that must be addressed if we are to move forward.

Walking around our town my husband and I are coming to appreciate the value of rocks in the garden, really big rocks. We see how rocks are becoming more important features in gardens, setting areas apart, defining boundaries, changing elevations and either providing a path or causing a direction change. Plants learn to live with them. Some snuggle close to rocks for protection. Others play paper, scissors, stone with them and climb right on top of them. Animals often create burrows where stone and plant meet. These big boys give the garden texture, reference points, and a backdrop upon which to shape beauty.

Pebbles, stones, rocks. Hard, unyielding, impossible to ignore and yet it is encountering them that we pause, get a different perspective and see how hard places can be opportunities to shape new beauty in the garden of our lives.

GOOD NEIGHBORS' HANDS

State Farm Insurance has the "like a good neighbor" commercial. Allstate reminds us that we are in good hands. I awoke this morning at 4:35 to a robin singing its song on the first day of summer. Apparently feeling no need for insurance with summer stretching and yawning in deliciousness, he sang an ode as leafy branches shook the remnants of last night's thunderstorm. And from now until September 21 we are summer folk. Unlike the robin, we divide life into bite size portions. We have ninety-one days to celebrate the good neighbors' hands that have tilled the soil, cared for crops and to enjoy the splendors of eye and tongue as summer unfolds her extravaganza.

Summers of my childhood were busy and idyllic times. My father toiled from morning to night, seven days a week. His good hands cooperated with nature to plant and grow crops, to care for and feed his cows. My mother was a gatherer, finding a use for anything nature offered. Her hands made wild grape juice from the grape vines that laced roadside trees. She picked tiny wild strawberries for what was arguably the world's best jam. Her scratched arms gathered blackberries and thimbleberries so we could dine like royalty on homemade ice cream topped with berries. Her garden yielded a menu of soups, salads and vegetables from April's asparagus to November's thick golden-fruited squashes. Apples, quinces, pears, cherries and peaches were a short step from the tree to the fruit jars neatly arranged on fruit shelves in the cellar.

Summers now have new concerns. The effluent in the Gulf of Mexico of fertilizer runoff from the Mississippi River now extends thirty to forty miles offshore. My idealized vision of good neighbors feeding the nation and the world has been tainted with murky algae that are suffocating aquatic life as twelve million tons of nitrogen fertilizers run off into the Mississippi basin extending into the Gulf, to an area roughly the size of New Jersey, creating a dead zone because the fish flee, as there is not enough oxygen for them and the rotting algae. The Gulf has become a fertilizer-enriched soup, disastrous for local fishermen, and now a third ingredient has been added, a huge dose of crude oil. The oil composed of hydrogen and carbon makes this soup a tasty treat for microscopic bacteria that munch on the free hydrocarbons from the Deepwater Horizon oil spill. We are brought into the world of interrelated ecosystems but good neighbors' hands in one context are raising havoc in another. What are we doing to summer's abundance? Is there warfare, not only between the farmers and the ranchers, but between ecosystems?

What will I tell the robin singing outside my window? My ode to summer will include pulling weeds, no fertilizers, cutting up vegetable waste for compost and trying to stretch for the summer blessings when, from naiveté or practice, life was more cooperative and good hands produced, maybe less, but certainly less damaging results. My father's farm was small and diverse by today's standards. Yet it yielded so many summer blessings. For instance, my father grew a field or two of peas for the local canning factory. I remember riding atop the truck with my dog the seven miles to the factory, but what I remember more vividly was sitting on the front porch on those June days when my father had cut the peas with my mother and we together would shell peas. They were so young and fresh that we would just pop them into our mouths. Supper those nights would be fresh homemade bread and sweet, sweet peas served in milk.

My father grew and butchered his own hogs and beef. Before electricity came that far out in the country my mother would can a whole cow in quart Mason jars. I was seven before I knew that beef was anything other than chunks that would fit inside those jars. Now we know too much beef can clog arteries and cause weight gain which further taxes the human heart.

So what has happened to my summers? Where are the good hands neighbors who tilled the soil, using what were believed to be best practices then? My mind's eye scanned the country roads I walked on, the amber fields of grain and the man and woman who lived their lives to bring food to our table and abiding love for the good earth that sustained us. Recently I walked down one of those roads of my youth where once stood a line of lush sugar maples that my father would tap in February. Now a single grey skeleton reminded me of time's relentless march. On that bare bones tree I counted thirteen bluebirds. Thirteen! In the theatre of my mind I recall what a boon DDT was to farmers after World War II. It was death to insects that munched and chewed the crops. But alas birds couldn't read and they still dined on grub, bug and worm who also couldn't read labels for toxic ingredients. When the momma and the papa bluebirds got together they produced soft shelled eggs that couldn't stand the rigors of even the fluffiest nursery. The maple tree died and stood as ghostly sentinel for a resurgence of bluebirds. As for my father and his DDT, Rachel Carson had quickened the consciousness of the silent spring as industry and agriculture began the search for less deadly pesticides.

In resurrecting hope the New York State Conservation Department taught farmers to build bluebird boxes. Bluebird homes started to appear on fence posts at about five foot levels, the birds' preferred nesting height. So decades later, walking familiar paths my heart sings, the bluebirds are back. Sky blue now has competition as they slash and wing on bright, windswept days.

Did I grow up with neighbors with good hands or with childhood's Pollyanna eyes? My father didn't know about bluebird eggs as he sprayed crops with DDT just as today we are learning the dire consequences of too much nitrogenous fertilizer runoff teaming up with hydrocarbons from a huge oil spill in the Gulf. But on Simmons Road in the town of Bristol thirteen bluebirds tipped their wings in testament to good neighbors who joined hands realizing that past mistakes can become occasions for rebirth and resurrection.

The destruction of our earth home gives rise to the question how can we creatures blessed with the crown of creation supersede the bluebirds and the fish in the Gulf of Mexico? Is it in nature's best interest to tilt the table by shortening the legs so that bounty runs into the laps of the few? Does personal security and insurance endanger the multitudes for generations to come? Where have all the flowers gone? Are the birds far behind? Think about it. What else do we have beside good neighbors who can work to ensure bluebird trees for another time?

I don't believe I was duped in my childhood. I am ready to sing of summer's glories for incredible diversity and the complex dance in the web of life. I am ready to join it. Good neighbors' hands are for shaping the good earth. We must become evangelists for a bright and healthy future.

The book of *Genesis* begins with these four words, "In the beginning God…" The book becomes a catalogue of human sinfulness. Very few behaviors distressing to God are excluded. After a complete and graphic list, in the fiftieth and last chapter we encounter Joseph, who has had been the special object of his brothers' scorn. They had sold him into slavery to get rid of their father's beloved pet. In reunion and reconciliation when his brothers need him, Joseph displays stellar knowledge of God's plan. An important official now in Pharaoh's court, Joseph tells his brothers, "Don't be afraid. Am I in place of God? You intended to harm me, but God intended it for good to accomplish what is now being done, the saving of many lives. So then do not be afraid, I will provide for you and your children" (Genesis 50:19-20 NIV). Those words seem to come directly from the Beneficent for our time. In turning, learning and reparations we may just come out right. That is God's insurance policy for his beloved creation. The good hands of a Great Neighbor.

NORTHERN GARDENER

Water Features

Garden magazines tout, and well-dressed gardens host, water features. A bubbling fountain, a babbling brook or a koi pond help to create an idyllic environment in which to find yourself relaxed or enthralled in wonder. At Peter the Great's summer palace in St. Petersburg, Russia there is a series of water features including a canal with a series of locks. The most amazing feature is a children's fountain section where waterspouts magically rise several feet out of the ground only to recede as another pops up. Children literally chase the waterspouts around the garden. This water feature was part of Peter the Great's rush to modernize Russia to the standards of the West. It is pure Disney a couple of centuries early. These fountains run entirely on the flow of gravity.

Our church garden has a modest water feature, also known as a bird bath. It used to be on the north side and alas, after repainting it several times I discovered it was placed right next to a sprinkler head, so its rusty façade was virtually guaranteed. This year I learned two things, well, three actually, about our water feature.

Deciding to move the water feature from the sprinkler head I found what would be an ideal location on the south side of the garden near the frangipani tree. I learned that it wasn't necessary to repaint. There is a product you can brush on the offending rust and it literally melts away. The bird bath, without the offending coppery crust, made the journey to the south side of the garden in the shade of the latticed wall.

All the time I was being observed. Two chatty blackbirds, feathers gleaming in the bright sunlight, were watching moving day with keen interest from their perch in the live oak trees. I could imagine their conversation back and forth.

> **One**: What in the world is she doing?
>
> **Other**: Don't know, this might be the most bizarre. I wish she would use another "toy" other than our beloved bath.
>
> **One**: Me too. You know it's been ages since I had a proper bath. It is always clogged with oak leaves and what little water in there is full of algae. It's hard to keep these iridescent feathers gleaming.
>
> **Other**: Look, she's moved it and now she's scrubbing it with a brush. This looks promising.

Their calls became more frequent and compelling as I rinsed the basin and put clear, life-giving water in their feature. They moved from the oak tree to the top of the wall for closer observation. No sooner was it filled than one flew down and took a bath.

This was a bath for the ages. He cavorted, dove, twisted, splashed, repeat. The other grackle waited somewhat patiently for him to finish. I put some more water in for the bath. I couldn't play favorites.

The take-aways from our relocated water feature:

1. Being too close to a sprinkler head can lead to rust.
2. There are sometime easier ways to deal with difficult problems than we can imagine.
3. Taking good care of our water feature produces benefits and joys beyond what we could have imagined.

Yes, and there was more learning. This week I noticed the bird's beloved bath is being filled with oak leaves from the live oak, this time on the south side of the garden. And the move? Well, there are sprinkler heads on the south side. I had placed the birdbath right on top of one! Water features can surprise us with unexpected joy but are part of a world that teaches humility as well.

MOTHER'S EARTH

This is my Mother's earth. She gives galaxies their birth
Noting smoke-filled skies, tending dying's cries
Her children have lost their worth.
This is my Mother's earth. Impatiently we wait.
When will we arise to nature's cries and hear the clear stream's mirth?

Fewer songs fill heaven's dome. Fewer species call earth home
What future waits behind hoarding gates, any hope for those unborn?
This is our Mother's earth, God knows how far we roam
Yet in our agony we can surely see
Troubled waters: shortest way home.

This is our Mother's world. And we her work of art
Within each part some of her good heart to make the future grow.
This is our Mother's world, sol'mnly nodding as we go
We make amends, call enemies, friends
And dance our intertwining part.

Writing alphabets of care, the forgotten start to dare
The meek inherit, the weak prepare it, to break bread everywhere.
This is our Mother's earth! Worn, tired, yet growing strong.
Fish swimming free, birds for every tree
Pilgrim choirs fill the air.

Election Day, 2020
Traditional English Melody, T*his Is My Father's World*

A FOX WENT OUT ON A CHILLY NIGHT

A fox went out on a chilly night and he prayed to the moon for to give him light
For he'd many a mile to go that night before he reached the town-o, town-o
He'd many a mile to go that night before he reached the town-o.

So she watched the fox with keen mind and wit, into silvery wood and out of it,
Pondering the ways of the hungry one before he'd reached the town-o, town-o, town-o
Pondering the ways of the hungry one before he'd reached the town-o.

She watched the fields at dusk and dawn, saw swoop of hawk and wobbly fawn,
Blankets of snow and coats of rain but the fox still moves to the town-o, town-o, town-o
Blankets of snow and coats of rain but the fox still moves to the town-o.

Flashing and darting through sunny field, 'til tip of tail was all the fox revealed
A glint, a glimmer, so much concealed the fox moves on to the town-o, town-o, town-o
A glint, a glimmer, so much concealed the fox moves on to the town-o.

Oh, the seasons come and the seasons go, life runs with force 'til the currents slows
Signals the fox and the watcher knows it's time to join the town-o, town-o, town-o

Signals the fox and the watcher knows it's time to join the town-o.

Lavender blooms in her side yard, trees stand tall her house to guard
Fox moves on though his way is hard for we must reach the town-o, town-o, town-o
Fox moves on though his way is hard for we must reach the town-o.

Verse 1 Folk Tune: A Fox Went Out on a Chilly Night
Elaine Eachus, 2010. Verses 2- 6 to honor the life of Donna Goodberlet

MAIL CALL

I lived on a dirt road about seven miles from town when I was a child. The arrival of the mailman everyday was a big deal. You could always tell an RFD (Rural Free Delivery) mailman seated in the middle of his front seat to expedite reaching to all those country mailboxes over deeply rutted approaches. The mailboxes might even be pockmarked by exuberant pre-adolescents taking target practice with their Daisy BB guns. Our mailbox on the farm was a gargantuan affair atop a post. It could easily hold a medium-sized dog. It had a red flag atop a metal arm which could be raised to notify the mail carrier that you have mail to go out that day. We could buy stamps or send packages with him. If my mother didn't have the right change to cover postage on a heavy envelope or a package she would put out a few dollars and the change would be returned in the same used envelope that my mother had attached to the package the day before. Times were simpler and mail was a primary method of communication for rural America.

Our farmhouse was a great distance from the road. The mailbox across the road. I was usually dispatched to bring in the mail. We did not receive much junk mail. People were not as eager to separate you from your money, or they may have correctly surmised, there was not a lot of money around those parts. But mail was important, and it connected us to each other and the world.

We would get letters from my mother's sisters and a sister-in-law. They filled us in on the health, achievements, struggles and joys in their families and would look forward to our get-togethers. Sometimes we would hear from friends and distant relatives and those letters were our entrée in their worlds and lives.

As a college student and then a newly-wed living 80 miles from home, my mother and aunt would write to me every week. In college they sent cookies. Their mail was a golden cord that meant I was connected to them though far away. Later in life, my dear Aunt Alice would send me letters written on tiny note pads from her nursing home. Sometimes she would just copy the daily devotional thought for the day. I knew I was cared for and remembered by those letters. Since my mother and aunt have both died, it's those letters I miss most. I guess it is a generational thing for my husband's mother, an only child, and her cousin, also an only child, wrote each other letters every week. As they got older the letters got shorter but I suspect it was a comforting touch for them as letters had been to our family.

Letters are now a few lines in a text, a one or two-word e-mail reply or something posted on Facebook. There is something about pen to paper that has nourished me since childhood. I miss that sweet communication. So imagine my joy when last Friday the letter carrier brought two hand-written letters to my door! The first was from my cousin, Evelyn, who had been instrumental in planning a family reunion for the descendants of my mother's parents, the Horace and "Sophie" Calkins family. Evelyn and her husband were trying to bring the Calkins genealogy up-to-date since Horace James Calkins and Mary Sophia Herendeen were married on Valentine's night, February 14, 1888 in Victor, New York.

In my memory, there was a cloud over my grandmother's life. There was a sadness surrounding my grandmother. I never met my grandmother. She died five years before I was born, and my grandfather, he died at the age of 47 in January 1912. His death must have brought incredible loss and sadness. My grandmother was left with six children. What must life have been like for her! Married women were housewives and mothers, as was she, and she now she was the sole breadwinner and parent for their six children. My mother, the third living child, was eleven at the time. The oldest, Uncle Marsh, must have been seventeen or eighteen, helped his mother. My mother would talk about her mother's sadness after her beloved Horace died. Mother remembered how her father could come in the house and tease his wife and the deep affection flowed between them. After he was gone, her mother never got her *joie de vivre* back. Somehow that sadness was transmitted through my mother for she was never seemed to be a particularly happy woman. I had seen formal portraits of my grandparents and true to their times those portraits are formal and somber. Not much hint of their personalities. I had never seen a picture of my grandparents in a natural life setting.

At the reunion Evelyn had brought a photo of my grandparents out in a field of wheat. My grandfather had straw hat pushed back on his elongating forehead, had his arm draped around his wife's shoulder and she was leaning toward him. Her hand rests on his shirt in warm intimacy. Somehow that photo captured such a natural moment in their lives and brought me so much joy and understanding of relationship they shared. Instantly I was connected to their warmth. I scanned it closely, for it provided a counterpoint to the sadness that clung so close, at least in my mother's memory. I asked Evelyn for a copy of that photo.

Mail call brought a copy of that ancient photo and in that same mail I received a gift to my future. Writing letters is not a habit of Generation Z, but there was a letter to me from one. The letter was from Emily, our oldest granddaughter. Emily just graduated from high school, doing well academically but finding her heart and passion on the soccer and lacrosse fields. My husband and I came to Florida for her graduation amid the most torrential downpour, even for Florida. We attended not only her graduation but got to see her team win a lacrosse tournament, again with the full accompaniment of rain which delayed the start of the second day's match almost three hours.

I was excited to read Emily's letter. I must confess that I have been prompting my grandchildren in the fine art of writing thank you notes. I have sent them stationery to prime the pump. I have written letters to suggest that a thank you note to a teacher or coach, in addition to brightening their day, will strengthen the positive memory when they ask for a letter of recommendation for college admission. Emily wrote that she was glad we shared that rainy graduation day.

> *Emily, I never knew any of my grandparents; you will never know what a privilege that day was for me! To be able to share your walking into your future and dreams, hopes and struggles is a gift beyond words. You will have your own path, but I will have witnessed the eighteen-year beginning. Such a tremendous joy.*

Together my husband and I have shared a lot of her life. I have memories, not secondhand memories like the photo of my grandparents taken over a hundred year ago. Sharing my grandchildren's lives is priceless. We have shared great things, everyday things, things that stick in the corners of my heart to treasure. I can pull those memories out and rejoice in the gift to the future our grandchildren will be. Imagine! In one mail call the grandparents I never knew and a grandchild who is starting her adult journey touched my heart with connections that wove the loveliest tapestry with threads from the past into the ribbons of the future.

A WORD ABOUT OUR COUNTRY

My Fellow Americans,
On the 244th anniversary of the signing of the Declaration of Independence I wanted to thank you for helping me become American. I thank you for showing me

... how tall we are when we stoop to help each other.
...how "me, my, mine" is really part of "we, our, ours."
...We are all Americans, there is no "they, them, theirs."
...that we have met the enemy and "they" is "us."
...a tilted playing field seeks the level where everyone can play their best game.
...that laughing at our own bravado heals malignant vanity.
...that how we do the small stuff is also how we do the big stuff.
...that we are as strong and healthy as the weakest among us, that is our social fiber.
...circling wagons make tight enclosures with little fresh air.
...life is full of paradoxes, larger circles make room to imagine other viewpoints and experiences.
...kids find so much fun in each adventure that they do not carry grudges.
...grudges are too heavy to lug around and waste too much time.
...discipline and restraint begin with me. That takes up all the complaint time in each day.
...the most amazing gifts of life are wrapped up in plain wrappers.
...discovering those gifts takes a lifetime of "attitude adjustment."
...picking up after myself can truly make America beautiful.
...our uncomfortable feelings easily get projected onto others when they are too difficult to own.

…that in this pandemic loneliness is a call to listen intently to the still, small voices within.
…the earth and everything in it is part of one community. Including us.

Thank you for teaching me so much. I am appreciative.

NORTHERNER GARDENER

Fences

This past week I had to tear out 20 feet on my garden along our driveway so that a carpenter could install three trellises to give us some privacy. Out came the foundation plantings of day lilies, the daffodils, the myrtle, the tulips, hydrangea, and iris! George, the carpenter, arrived and built the trellises Monday afternoon. Tuesday my husband and I planted the new autumn clematis which will hopefully climb the trellises and by September reach the top and have created a mass of ethereal white feathery, fragrant blossoms that will cover the trellises to give visual separation between the two houses. Yesterday I put in four new varieties of day lilies and some of old ones, the iris, the allium, and daffodil bulbs. The tulips are going in the back garden. I added some portulaca, dianthus, and white coneflowers, finishing up just as it started to rain.

What a gift from God! That gentle rain lasted a couple of hours, giving the plants a welcoming shower in their new or transplanted home. I reposition the black iron crane between the trellises so he, too, now peers out on this strip garden. I cannot hide my enthusiasm. I must have looked out on that garden thirty times yesterday afternoon to see how the plants are responding to the change. Is the clematis taller, is the portulaca sporting new buds, the dianthus blooming?

Gardening is like faith. We plant but we can't control the variables. Some plants may not make it. The kids next door could hit a hard ball through the screen on the trellis or a branch punch a hole in one of them. But we will never know unless we try. The plants may die, and there may be wonderful surprises and delights. On our refrigerator there is a magnet that says, “Bloom where you are planted.” I’m hoping my new garden will take that advice seriously. In the meantime, I will water and fertilize, and rejoice when God waters because rain water is supposed to be better for plants than hose water. And I will trust that the garden will reveal God’s amazing technicolor landscape and create sacred spaces for our families to dwell in privacy. In the meantime, the God of abundance has given me tons of day lilies to give to my friends and the remainder I will put on the curb in plastic grocery bags for strangers to take home and try their hand with them.

How does your garden grow? Does your garden need to be modified? Does your garden need boundaries just like we do to function well? Too much a good thing? New growth needed for the rest of your life? Is your garden like mine? Do you need to thin the beds, sort and separate, create a little privacy, get rid of some things so God can do magic in your heart and garden?

AWAITING THE HURRICANE

Job lamented, Handel composed, I saw---
Though worms destroy this body, yet in my flesh shall I see God.
Jesus foretold it, Wendell Berry amended it, I considered it---
Birth, growth, maturity, death, and decay on both sides of the cross.

A flowering maple tree, seedling, sprout, sapling, spindly
thickening stem, three yellow buds, a golden crown, discarded remnants
harden into wooden dreidels littering the patio, birds sample, bees croon
green to golden leaves leave, thick, sinewy, strewn.

Internal stress, a root severed, arboreal gout, small fissure widened,
lengthened, deepened. A lifeless branch grew, spread, cancer-like.
Spinning, orbiting, skeletal remains on the tree of life--- twigs snap,
birds rest, launch; some preen---zebra longwings pas de deux among the
dead branches.

Summer sets in; lifeless limbs are now flight decks to dragonflies, platoons
of dragonflies, biplanes of color- first the gossamer blues;
next the carnival yellow and rusty striped. Now Red Barons flying with their signature circles of ocher. The drill is the same; they all face Mecca with bodies poised and wings ready, spaced like Italian lights on a Christmas tree---
exquisite, sheer.

Except this once: frenzied winds playing tag, leapt down on the platoon.
Turning as one, menacing, they faced due west: hurricane averted.
Job lamented, Handel soared, I saw: Though worms destroy this body
yet in my flesh shall I see God.

August 1, 2020, awaiting Isaias

LISTENING

I felt the wind rush by my side
I thought I heard God's call
I chose a star and set my path
But did I hear God at all?

Chorus:
I want to know need you to tell me
The path to freedom and love
I want to hear your voice
Feel my heart rejoice
O God, I need to know.

I saw the lightning fill the sky
The thunder shook the ground.
I cried, "God, I will wait for you.
But the silence made no sound.

Fiery tongues danced around me now
Swirling in garb of red.
But only in the quietness
Can God's own word be said.

Pilgrim, now stop your frantic pace.
Rest, lean your care on me.
I choose and call and give my grace,
And in my time, I set free.

Worship at ACTS Summer 1996
Elaine Eachus Words and Music.

THE SONG OF SILENCE

Just when we sense our purpose, just when we hear life's call
It's then we're lost and groping, it's then darkness will fall.
In the midst of all our sureness; in the midst of our schemes tall
That the music we have danced to is no music we recall.

When all the things we have stood for, when all we thought was so true
Why God, your total silence, after all that we've been through?
Can it be we failed to follow, how has our love been untrue?
Then it's silence, lonely silence, not the music that we knew.

Hush! Now it's the time of waiting, it's the time to bless the dark
You stand still, assured and proud ones, and you watch for one small spark
A new day will soon be breaking, in the darkness, listen! Hark!
Stand still, for God will turn you, listen for the morning lark.

In the time of quiet waiting and in the time of watching too
It's then God will move us to horizons bold and new
It's God's silent preparation; hid from our imperfect view
Here's the song of lovely silence with God's whispers breaking through.

For Terry
Hymn Tune: Natalie Sleeth, "Hymn of Promise"

NORTHERN GARDENER

Maintenance

One of the thankless tasks in gardening is maintaining it. This isn't the thrill of new pops of color. Pulling weeds seldom rates a line in a gardening magazine. Cutting back shrubs or trees when they've stepped out of bounds is hardly a blip on the screen of gardening joy, and my personal nemesis for Florida is raking leaves in the spring. That chore was devised as an alternative to purgatory. Those thick, leathery leaves are a nasty detour from enjoyment of the serenity of a garden. It is all work and no play that breaks my back. There must have been some breakdown in communications when God assigned humankind the role of maintaining the garden. Is that how Adam and Eve got in trouble, forgetting to rake the leaves from the tree of knowledge of good and evil?

I wasn't designed for drudgery. Let me "oh and ah" at each emerging rosebud. I will join the choirs of delight as the frangipani goes from naked to crowns of spring glory worthy of the loveliest lei. Bird songs in the air and patterns of leaves dancing in the sunlight are my thing. Why, oh why, is it my lot to pick up the tossed water bottle, the cellophane that blew in from the street or carelessly tossed cigarette butts?

Marie Kondo's 2014 book, *The Life Changing Magic of Tidying Up,* gives us a fresh approach. The author says that mindset is the cornerstone of the process. The goal is a positive relationship with the things that bring us joy. We need to get rid of what is no longer needed in our lives. Is there that same sense of purpose in the garden? Is there a relationship between my dirty knees and fingernails and the delight I find when the creeping jenny tumbles over the edge of a pot of petunias to amaze me?

This is the month of Arbor Day and Easter. The former celebrates the gift of trees and their role in God's beautiful earth and the latter embraces God's beautiful gift of creation and the relationship in which God holds us and all of creation. Jesus lived so that we could see first-hand how to live in the relationship of love that God has for his children. Then the most amazing thing happens. We can see how to maintain ourselves when it seems like we are losing, stuck as the clean-up crew in a garden inhabited by out-of-control behaviors of all who live there or pass by.

As we understand our role in the garden, we are given time to see between the weeds, the dead flowers, and overgrown bushes that an amazing drama is being revealed. Maintaining our garden is the way we stay in relationship with the Ground of Being, as Paul Tillich calls God. The monotony and drudgery of the same old, same old familiarizes us with the myriad of activity and growth that happens virtually imperceptibly. I never can take the garden in all at once. There is always something new to behold and wonder about. That is the mystery of growth, particularly Easter growth. How did we miss that the Risen Christ nudging us to see our relationship with God and creation? How did we overlook those few dead looking twigs yesterday which have tiny green buds on them today?

In Mark's gospel the Easter story ends with the women entering the tomb and a young man dressed white tells them that Jesus is no longer there. But he commands them, to tell the disciples and Peter to go back to Galilee and there they will see him, just as he told you. Why, Galilee? That is where the disciples did their life's work as fishermen and disciples of Jesus. So, despite my protests I must get back to the garden, to trudge on. It is not because of some assignment as a wretched sinner. I am one of God's beloved children, just as you are. It is because in the garden of our lives we will find the incredible---beauty, joy and peace when we finally get the hang of our role and relationship with God. Then I can truthfully announce that there is no place I would rather be!

WATCH YOUR LANGUAGE!

This morning as I walked out of the gym a tall trainer was greeting an acquaintance. "My life is really goin' great," he said, smiling broadly. "Now if I could get just get rid of my partner who is a total @! * and it would be perfect." In that moment I could imagine my mother planted firmly before this wonderfully fit specimen of humanity, looking up at him and saying, "Young man, watch your language."

My mother was precise about language and particularly using good grammar. She would correct our grammatical errors and insist we take Latin in high school to see how words function in the community of a sentence. Cussing was beyond the pale of polite human discourse. Swearing was a direct violation of the fourth commandment as any Methodist should know.

Mother died in 1993 and even as her mental capacities were diminishing, she would still blanche when the "the king's English," as she called it, was violated. Maybe it was a generational thing, for her sister, my Aunt Alice, told me early on to be careful how I talked about my siblings, "for anyone who calls his brother a fool is in danger of hell's fire." (Mt 5:22 KJV). That did it for me. I never called my brother, or sisters, for that matter, a fool. It seemed miniscule to me, but I didn't want to go to hell. I called them much worse things, I'm sure.

Today we speak differently. The speaker is number one and signals a worldview change. No longer would we say, "Mary and I did something," but "me and Mary did something." The subject no longer shows deference to the other, instead placing himself in the position of honor. If our language does present the microcosm of our worldview, and "as a man thinketh in his heart so is he" (Proverbs 23:7 KJV), then we have moved into another dimension. As the age of enlightenment fades and the digital age brings millennials with demanding fingers for Amazon and Uber Eats a few clicks away we can see ourselves in a different context. We have moved into a beck and call world.

But standing on the cusp of this new reality I realize, like Moses and Martin Luther King, Jr., I may not make it to the promised land. I look at some of the signposts that marked my journey so far.

The Good Old Days

In the old days greater care was given to the written and spoken word. It was honored. With fewer instantaneous distractions it seemed that more time was given to reflect on the power of the word to capture and elevate the experience of the community. School children memorized great speeches and passages of the ages, often in their original language. Beautiful words from religious sources could be recited by the faithful gathered. Words shaped a communal understanding.

But many things fell outside the pale of correctness. These were not discussed and great was the suffering of those aggrieved. Language served as a social barrier. The Liza Doolittles of the world were ostracized as soon as they opened their mouths. It was another criterion of who's in.

Language is a container for larger life. Metaphor intimates the divine. Words delve the recesses of our desires, pain, and longings, help frame and give voice to our humanity. As music illuminates experience beyond words, the beautiful words hold us in a community beyond the border of "me, my, mine." Singing invites us to participate in those angel choirs. Today's great reluctance to sing in public is like our sellout to professional athletes. We would rather have performers do our work. Using the gifts of body and voice for the glory of God and our own health and enjoyment takes a back seat to having a professional do it for us, yet we jealously guard our own front seat to our likes, dislikes, and criticisms.

New Realities

Democratization of the word opened it to colloquialism and infusion of other languages. Technical, digital, and pop culture moved in and began speaking in tongues which generally the young were the first to appropriate into their vocabularies.

In the burgeoning sea of language, expressing our thoughts quickly, in knee jerk time, takes precedence over deliberation, awareness of others and consequences of our words. Twitter and Facebook remove the filters of discretion from the human equation. Fact checking is reserved for newspaper reporters long after Pandora's box has been opened.

Ken Burns in his PBS documentary on the Vietnam War, quotes a Marine veteran John Musgrave who explains how failing to watch our language erodes our soul and we lose our birthright as sons and daughters of God. Musgrave recounts:

> I only killed one human being in Vietnam, and that was the first man I ever killed. I was sick with guilt about killing that guy and thinking that I'll have to do this for the next 13 months, I'm gonna go crazy. And I saw a marine step on a Bouncing Betty mine, and that's when I made my deal with the devil, in that I said, "I will never kill another human being as long as I'm in Vietnam. However, I will waste as many gooks as I can find. I'll wax as many dinks as I can find. I'll smoke as many zips as I can find---but I ain't gonna kill anybody."[45]

How do we get to that point of agency where another's humanity is an object of our manipulation? The distance from our words and their effect and losing our humanity by denying it to another is a short step. "Young

[45] Musgrave quote in Ken Burns and Lynn Novick, *The Vietnam War,* volume 1, episode 5. https://www.washington*post.com/news/act-four/*wp2017/09/22/the-american-war-why-you-need-to-understand-american-racism-to-understand-what-happened-in-vietnam/-362k

man, watch your language." But what if we hit the pause button for a moment and retrace our steps and see what is hidden within ourselves we understand the connection between history of our past wounding and how we function today. For every time we open our mouths and frame our thoughts in words we are creating ourselves, who we are and who others are in relation to ourselves. And for better or for worse, we create our children verbally too. We all abhor child abuse; it revolts us. Yet unconsciously we abuse children with words that label and stigmatize the most precious gifts we can give the world. Verbal abuse can run deep and leave lasting scars.

A Child Shall Lead Them

Harville Hendrix and Helen Hunt's book, *Giving the Love that Heals* helps parents grow in awareness of their life story and move into well-being while helping their children over the rough spots in their lives. Their approach has value for anyone who senses the disquieting within and longs to bring a harmony to the many voices pitched in a murderous scream. Shelves of books have been written on communication techniques, but I chose this one because it begins with the fact that we have an innate desire to nurture a bit of the universe to well-being and wholeness. Their communication technique is called intentional dialogue. Making this a part of a toolkit for touchy situations may then spill over into our everyday conversations. It can become a fulcrum to discover ourselves, our history of neediness and the way forward with our child, and to healing conversation with others. Intentional dialogue begins with listening and checking that you have indeed heard correctly what the other is saying. Secondly, you let the other person know you acknowledge their feelings and, thirdly, you try to feel or understand what the other is feeling. You're probably thinking how naïve that communication techniques could move us into new understandings with the intractable problems of our time, political climate, and gridlock, but listening may be the first act of love. [46]

---

[46] Harville Hendricks and Helen Hunt, *Giving the Love that Heals* (NY: Pocket Books,1997) 248.

Pundits are telling us that the various scenarios for moving forward must include everything in the universe from neutrinos to those who feel they have been left behind and the train has already left the station. Feelings are often the forgotten component, which, when honored, become the docents to the way forward. "Wasting gooks," "waxing dinks," and "smoking zips" are encountered as the unbearable stain of human emotions before they become concretized as the way of life in the jungle. What would mass murderers, school shooters and radicalized assassins discover if they had been listened to, heard, and had explored these overpowering feelings?

Hendrix and Hunt talk about growing in interpersonal relationships with the children. When adults become aware of the barriers they have developed to protect themselves from harm and pain of childhood and an out-of-control world, they can move into healthier relationships. It is a tough passage.[47]

Dismissing the Loyal Soldier

In *Falling Upward* Richard Rohr relates the story of discharging the loyal soldier. After World War II Japanese communities understood that the returning soldiers had spent their lives being good soldiers for the Emperor. They were not prepared to enter the life of the community. A ritual was created to integrate them into the community to become something more than a soldier. There were elaborate thank yous and public accolades for bravery and service. This was done at great length. Then "The war is over!" the community cried. "The community needs you to let go of what has served you and us well up to now. We need you to return as a man, a citizen and something beyond being a soldier." He received a harsh slap on the face.[48]

Maturing beyond the peril of childhood and dismissing our loyal soldier means finding the courage to face our wounds and past actions. When we transcend their power in our lives, our fears can be marshalled to become

[47] _______, 136.

[48] Richard Rohr, *Falling Upward* (San Francisco: Jossey-Bass, 2011) 43-44.

the listening, empathetic, and compassionate ears who hear their child or another's worldview. Parents want to help their children grow into healthy adults. The parent who confronts his/her deepest fears discovers a deep reservoir of well-being. Here there is *shalom,* a peace, that religious texts tell us, passes human understanding.

As a pastor I have been privileged to bury many of Tom Brokaw's *Greatest Generation* veterans. Some families would tell me their loved ones never talked of their military experiences, some would mention it in passing. But the families knew if the experience was an emotional minefield where their loved one trod carefully so as not to detonate a booby trap, or another part of life that had been woven into the tapestry of days. I hoped that it would have been the latter, but always fervently prayed that God would grant them all peace. I believe that giving the love that heals by first working on our own life offers a wonderful shot at it.

Healing the Breach

While this is just one method to understanding how healing communication begins with each of us, I chose *Giving the Love that Heals* for its implicit underlying good will and hope for good outcomes for the children whom we cherish. Because so much of language begins with the attack and devolves into negative and degrading speech, rooting relationships in good will places our discussion on a plain where horizons are more open and vistas inviting.

Watching our language gives us the hope that consciousness is better than unconsciousness, and self-reflection can move us forward. Mindfulness is the buzz word for looking within through meditative practices and exercises to help us understand how the parts of us create the dynamic connections among all things. We understand that dynamic and changing relationships evolve and become part of larger systems while the seemingly insignificant parts of human experience exist within each of us and they create huge energy vortexes within us.

These tumultuous times and the yawning canyons that divide call forth Lincoln's "better angels." That distance between us and others has given permission to attack and debase those we find on the other side of the divide. Hendrix and Hunt observed that giving the love that heals begins with healing the giver. In stretching to see and hear where the child is "caught" they can relate through the vehicle of their own experiences in childhood. In fact, the child's problem is a huge gift to the parent for it reveals exactly where the parent had become stuck in his/her childhood. Dealing with their own material frees up the parent to grow beyond the very place where the child/parent dynamic is stuck is exactly the place where the parent needs to work.[49] The bravado, the anger, withdrawal, turning away of the child is where the heavy lifting of relationship needs to take place first within the adult. The adult must be willing to look closely at the log in his/her own eye before going after the speck in another's eye, as Jesus reminded us.

Up Ahead

The focus is not on addressing old hurts but moving forward together toward a future with greater mindfulness and awareness. Using the authors' metaphor, the parent and child are held in the same orbit together. Hendrix and Hunt suggest that there is an attraction, an energy that holds them regardless of the size of their orbit. Watching language mindfully means that we can explore the power within that orbit. Good self-care requires attention to spiritual, physical, and mental health. Angry language, emotional eruptions, rage are tipoffs that the orbit of connection has found a place that needs our attention so that the orbit will flow and grow.

Watch your language is a wake-up call to check what is going on within. Martin Buber sees the beauty of each of us is a part of the cosmos. We belong together in a mysterious and holy way. We are to honor the whole and each part, you and me, the I and Thou. We are spun back to creation where God noticed each part: it was good. The enormity of that goodness

---

[49] Hendrix and Hunt, 165.

brings us to a moment of awe: the magnificence of our creation on the third planet from the sun.

Our maturation and healing do not happen in a vacuum. We need structures and strategies that will encourage and enhance this healing of how we relate as children of this universe. Twenty years ago, James Robertson wrote about what was blowing in the wind. In his book, *Beyond the Dependency Culture*, Robertson contends we need sustainable political policy. It will involve shifting emphasis: toward ends away from means; away from quantitative towards qualitative values and goals; away from impersonal, from organizational goals toward personal and interpersonal; and away from the earning and spending of money towards the meeting of real human needs and aspirations. A culture that has been masculine, aggressive, and domineering in its outlook will give place to one which is more feminine, cooperative, and supportive. A culture that has exalted the uniformly European will give way to one which values the multi-cultural richness and diversity of human experience. An anthropocentric worldview that has licensed the human species to exploit the rest of nature as if from above and outside it, will give place to an ecological worldview. We shall recognize that survival and self-realization alike require us to be as what we really are: integral parts of an ecosystem much larger, more complex, and more powerful than ourselves.[50]

I wonder if life would be any different in the great scheme of things if that trainer had walked out of the gym and acknowledged his life was great and he was going to have to do some growing in his relationship with his partner. Watching our language can be the start of reshaping ourselves. That just might be the biggest task on planet earth.

---

[50] James Robertson, *Beyond the Dependency Culture: People, Power and Responsibility* (Westport, CT: Praeger Publications, 1998) 90.

COPS AND ROBBERS

Cops become robbers
and strong arm the witnesses
who become liars for the bribes
and are soon the enforcers
protecting the king who is proudly
wearing the emperor's new clothes
as the crowds cheer.

Oh God, such a dirty business and what starts out noble, pure, and hopeful soon lies, trampled like a Subway wrapper, and I am tired, too dissolute to pick it up. Will I be arrested for littering or loitering?

Idolatry and adultery come from the same root word; both signifying a break in our own sacredness as we were created. We have lost a sense of belonging, a context where, whatever our gift, it can be a part of a greater whole, where we are beloved by God.

Complete in God's eyes keeps us content and humble in the vastness of the universe. To be a rock in the garden, a simple grey stone bears testimony to billions and billions of years of creativity swirling. And now to find our context is to find beauty. That seems a silly notion that beauty is a panacea for violence. Yet finding self in the garden is to feel the convulsion of creation, a time of cooling, eons of ice, warmed by the sun and baptized through the eternity by the rain, river and ocean.

AMERICAN EDUCATION AND ME: A CONFESSION

Of all the angers and frustrations resulting from the COVID 19 pandemic the abuses at the expense of American public-school children make me most angry. My rage reached the boiling point when revelations of the widespread abuses of the government's opening its checkbook perpetrated further disparity for our poorer children.

The Coronavirus Aid, Relief and Economic Security (CARES) Act and the Paycheck Protection Plan (PPP) were two pieces of hastily thrown together legislation passed to help ease the horns of the dilemma: the coronavirus pandemic and the economic meltdown. Their effect, in actuality, was widening the gulf between America's poorer children in economically and racially segregated areas while those voices of the powerful and rich were heard in the legislative corridors and their outstretched hands received a disproportionate amount of what was meant to prop up communities that have borne the load inflicted upon the poorer and racially vulnerable communities.

How did this happen? Congress approved CARES, $13.5 billion to help public schools in low-income districts to create pathways for online distance learning with attendant technology for their students. The bill's intent was to aid public schools in poorer districts caught in the disparity gap.[51] But the Secretary of Education Betsy De Vos' interpretation was that the funds had to be distributed equally among all children attending public or private school in the district. Billions of dollars were funneled from the poor districts into private schools; the amount originally designated

[51] "Stolen Education," *The Christian Century,* 137 no.16, July 29, 2020, 7.

for private schools was $127 million. With the DeVos' interpretation it soared to $1.5 billion.[52] That meant children in lower income districts would be further disadvantaged as more funds were removed from their already-hurting funding; more money to schools who needed it less. If anyone wondered how trickle-down economics works for public education, you could check the dry spigot for poorer districts. Check their lower test scores, with further reduction in funding for children in these areas, it is easy to blame the victim.

But that was only part of the hijack. The Paycheck Protection Plan was another entree for private education intended to keep small businesses afloat including small private schools and private preschools. The eligibility for PPP is that the applicant must employ less than 500 people, be a small business, sole proprietor, independent contractor, self-employed person, 501 (c) (3) non-profit organization, 501(3)(19) veterans' organization, or tribal business. The further restriction was a net worth of less than $15 million and an average net income that did not exceed $5 million for the two previous fiscal years. And oh yes, the loan was totally forgivable if no one was laid off.[53]

But those who love sausage and the law should not be present when either is being made. Enter the cloakroom where the slicing and dicing commences. Religious groups persuaded the Trump administration to allow them access to the funds even if they had more than 500 workers. Without this preferential treatment many Catholic dioceses would have been ineligible to apply for PPP, as between the head offices, parishes, schools and affiliates they would exceed 500 employees.[54] This government's structural dispensation creates favoritism, and that favoritism was worth billions of dollars. For, in addition, the Catholic and private schools only had to report a range of the handout they received from the federal government *and* were not accountable for how the funds were spent. The public schools were accountable. Private schools had outstretched hands and tightly sealed lips.

---

52 ibid.

53 https://en.wikipedia.org/wiki/Paycheck Protection Program

54 Reese Dunklin and Michael Rezendes, "After getting exemption, Catholic Church received at least $1.4 billion in PPP loans," *Miami Herald*, July 14, 2020, 7A.

In Miami the Ransom Everglades School (no kidding, that is their name) has an endowment of $40 million and charges $41,700 yearly tuition. The Ransom Everglades headmaster makes $410,000 while, as a means of comparison, the Miami-Dade County Public School superintendent leads 392 schools with 345,000 students and makes $363,000. Private schools only are required to reveal the parameters of their loan. Ransom Everglades received between $2 and $5 million dollars; no further discussion or accountability required.[55]

As a result of this exception, public school students received far less than the intent of the legislation because private schools within their district got an undisclosed loan with no accountability. The Catholic entities benefitted heavily, receiving about 9,000 loans nationwide, making them one of major beneficiaries in the PPP.[56] To be fair, the PPP has also benefited companies of members of Congress, professional sports teams, large corporations, and governors. But PPP was a gift to dioceses that have spent millions of dollars in the past few years for sexual abuse settlements. The United States Conference of Catholic Bishops, both lobbied for the PPP and does not keep track of what the dioceses received or how the funds were spent. One irony however is that St. Luke Institute in Maryland received a loan ranging from $350,000 to $1,000,000. St. Luke Institute has been a way station at times for priests accused of sexual abuse who returned to active ministry only to abuse again.[57]

Now, in 2020, a crack has become a chasm. The PPP gives those private schools a chance to gobble up what was initially touted as a lifeline for the average citizen and small business. How does that work? Congress let faith groups tap into the PPP, the fund created to keep Main Street open and Americans employed. Then Congress sweetened their largess with a cherry on the top: they would be given a further exception from the rule that typically disqualified an applicant with more than 500 employees. This exemption meant that many Catholic dioceses with more than 500

[55] Fabiola Santiago, "COVID PPP loan grab by private and charter schools is wrong," *Miami Herald,* July 23, 2020, 3A.

[56] Dunklin and Rezendes, Ibid.

[57] ibid.

employees could exceed the cap. But cherries go better on a mountain of whipped cream so the caveat that private schools do not have to be accountable for how the loans are spent is a blank check for whatever. There is no oversight as there is with the public schools.[58] The First Amendment groans under the weight of exceptionalism.

Do No Harm

How could something designed to alleviate suffering of the pandemic and the economic downturn become another wedge between the haves and the have nots? And how could the notion of public education become the cudgel for those who point to public education as a failed American experiment? The Founding Fathers had experienced the chaos in Europe when the state hopped in bed with the church. Clearly, they did not intend the two to become as one. But some legal experts contend that the special consideration the government has given with PPP has further eroded the wall between church and state to a translucent membrane by granting religious groups that do not pay taxes special access to public money.

Now a global pandemic reveals profound stress fractures in the current epoch of the American experiment. Our schools have often been a convulsive battleground about reigning American values. In my lifetime we moved from one-room schoolhouses to desegregating schools, to busing, to affirmative action, to the post-Sputnik-responses, to charter schools, to tuition vouchers for private education, to a "dead end," as Secretary of Education describes American public education and has devoted most of her time to undermining that public trust.[59] In June 2020, a Supreme Court ruling further weakened the membrane between taxpayers supporting religious education by ruling states must give religious schools the same access to public funding that other private schools receive. [60]

[58] Santiago, ibid.

[59] "Stolen Education," ibid.

[60] "Supreme Court Lifts Ban on Aid to Religious Schools," *The Christian Century*, 137 no.16, July 29, 2020, *14-15*.

The notion that the government has the responsibility to provide the best schooling possible for its children so that they in turn would become the best citizens possible for that country was a precious tenet that got subsumed in the rush to promote the idea that rugged individualism was worth far more than a rising tide that could raise all boats. Using what we discovered about individual differences and trying to meet those needs became distorted and ugly, a caricature of fuzzy thinking and watered-down education. To truly educate our children we needed *standards*, no child left behind. Quantifiable, spreadsheet, bottom line hard statistics. Child in, follow regimen, educated child out. And the private education Greek chorus lamented, "You are doing it all wrong. There is another way, full of our values, full of right-thinking people, people who can prove our success by how we have risen to become the cream of the crop. We can do much better than what you set out to do and have failed, even by your own standards."

I taught for 20 years. I grew up in a family of teachers, my great aunt, my mother, my aunt, my sister, and my nephew stand in that line. When it was my turn, I suddenly veered from my training as a journalist and became a teacher. What a trial by fire that was! My first year utterly exhausted me, I was so ill-prepared, so lacking in confidence. I said I should have paid my students for letting me practice. But what we discovered was together, as students and teacher rode out the storms of my learning curve, that each year by the luck of the draw, we would socialize each other that year. And each one of us would do it, probably unintentionally, and that would be part of what each of us needed to become whole at that time.

The Secret of Our Success

Perhaps it was my desperation that set my eyes casting for any clues to make my own educational experiment work. Perhaps it was the experience of growing up in a rural America where I was known by my teachers and knowing that there was a network of information shared within the community, especially with my parents. Maybe it was the agrarian understanding of hard work being necessary for a good harvest. Maybe it was the great reverence my parents carried for the sacrifices of those who came before. Looking back over decades I carry treasures from that context into today. It shaped me. It was the place where America's children could enter in the American experience. It was the responsibility that the society pledged themselves to continue the blessings of the American experience for our posterity, each generation's pledge to the next: a community where each is an equal participant. Public education was and is America's future, the ongoing creation and responsibility of the American community.

Our grandchildren in Virginia and Florida have had that education and cultural experience as their schools reflect a greater diversity and multicultural blending than we or their parents had. While moving further into technological and post-modern education needed for the future, the notion that it takes a village to raise a child is the cornerstone of our educational commitment.

How Change Is Possible

A man told his doctor of his wife's hearing loss. "She just can't hear anymore," he lamented. The doctor told him to test her hearing by going to the farthest room in the house and calling, "What's for dinner?" Keep moving closer to her until she is finally able to hear you. He does just what the doctor ordered. Finally, standing just outside the kitchen he called to her. Angrily, his wife answered, "For the fifth time, chicken." We just cannot imagine there could be another reality other than the one we have constructed.

But we are products of our time and we assume those constructs are normative. We tinker with the components within, as the Enlightenment taught us, but seldom question if we have understood the context accurately and fully. The mystics remind us that creation is all inclusive, the good, the bad, the ugly. Rumi, a Sufi mystic (1207-1273 CE), surprises us with a context that leaves nothing out, not our worst enemy, nor any cataclysmic events. Rumi takes us to the new ground beyond our determinations. He said, "Beyond right or wrong, there is a field. I will meet you there." Beyond my belief and your stubbornness there is a field where all is included, in its messiness, its wonder, its growth, death and decay, and its potential to transform into new life. This field subsumes our geo-centric and helio-centric notions of time and space in a new understanding of the vast cosmos wherein a medium sized star burns in one galaxy, will die, and the vastness of creation will continue its evolution. That is a lot to take in. We are frequently stuck outside the kitchen waiting to be heard.

The mystics tell us what we have selectively thrown out is part of the cosmos that does not suit our worldview. Brené Brown, says in *The Power of Vulnerability,* that religion has gone from belief in a mystery to a certainty: "I am right, you are wrong. That is it."[61] And then somewhat sanctimoniously we add, "Here I stand, so help me, I can do no other." We certainly impede the creation of a new heaven and a new earth which prophets have foretold through the ages. The long-awaited field where we can meet will just have to wait a while longer until we can get past our right and your wrong.

Up Close and Personal

As I shared my experience of American public education, I want to share what my side of the right/wrong debate looks like. My proclivities put me in the progressive/liberal camp. I am always cheering for the underdog. I got that trait from my father: he was a friend of those who were on the bottom of the social heap. He enjoyed poking holes at the bluster and bravado of those who were full of themselves. My life's experience has made me suspicious. I am always looking around to see who has the power. That comes in part from my training as a journalist, in part from my angry feminism of the 60s, and being somewhere between a NINE and a ONE on the Enneagram. My birthdate placed me in the Enlightenment where I look for what is wrong and how to fix it. The question of serving, participating in the mystery, runs a distant second to my proclivity to rearrange or mentally improve things in my head. I am suspicious, confident in my opinions and judgments, and cynical about the motives of others.

---

[61] Brené Brown, *The Power of Vulnerability audiobook*, Sounds True Publisher, 2012.

Richard Rohr in his book, *What the Mystics Know,* says every cynic was once an idealist who just could not find happiness in this broken world and took refuge in the theatre of his mind. The world never measured up. Living in this broken world and still working for its reform is beyond their ken. They especially shun authority structures. They have caught the dis-ease of their own liberalism. They are neither good leaders nor good followers because their knee jerk reaction is to mistrust power and leadership itself. But good leadership is necessary for real change; yet liberalism is all about maintaining personal and social freedom. Their groups quickly deconstruct because a highly opinionated self quickly will come in conflict with another's freedom and the structure will soon collapse.[62]

For Heaven's Sake

From my ivory tower, looking down, I cannot fully understand nor participate in the companionship and help that binds those who walk on the often-treacherous paths of humanity with all its messiness and stumbling blocks. The ability to laugh at myself and get over some of my priggishness may put me on course to participate in an imperfect social structure with imperfect constituents trying to help each other reach that kingdom, which we have been assured, is at hand. By hanging together our vulnerability removes our fear. Acknowledging weakness makes clowns of those who risk derision to journey with others who have their crosses and failures to claim. That is a paradoxical state until we get it. When we do get it, we will be home and know the place for the first time. The apostle Paul spilled a lot of ink trying to get early communities in the first century Roman Empire trying to understand that.

"Here I Stand"

I am a cautious type. My style is to hug the tree but not to go too far out on the limb. Here is my confession: I believe that to fulfill my

[62] Richard Rohr, *What the Mystics Know, (*NY: Crossroad Publishing, 2015) 22-23.

citizenship I must be willing to give up my "I'm right and you're wrong" assumptions and work on the issues with humility. This is much harder than complaining about all that is wrong. I must imagine new ways to live in harmony within the cosmos. I must do the excruciating work of waiting and watching, holding my tongue, seeing myself as a part of the problem. A small rock working free can start an avalanche. The environmentalists tell us we cannot just do one thing. But the loneliness of this process feels like the dark night of the soul, unyielding and shapeless while the new is incubating. I must be willing to change my faulty perceptions; in the very areas where I am most vulnerable, I must find the gold within the tons of dross. Those judgments that I have honed to quick perfection must cease and desist while I look to see what is going on with others. What are *their* perceptions, hurts, and growing edges? Foremost, what do they have to teach me? How do they see American education? What can respectful sharing yield?

I am hoping that my voice does matter. I believe American public education is the vehicle by which we, as citizens of this republic, have the privilege and responsibility to raise each succeeding generation with finest wisdom, resources, teachers, and mentors to be sure the tree of life flourishes in this country. I must do my difficult task and keep trudging toward that field that Rumi told us about where we meet each other in our humanity and humbly walk together into the future.

NORTHERN GARDENER

Weeds

Weeds are garden volunteers. One definition of a weed is a plant growing in the wrong place. Weeds are part of the landscape. No one intentionally plants weeds, they are just there--- wind-blown, airborne, bird refuse, attached to a person or animal, they just arrive and intrude. They even hide in ridiculously expensive bags of garden soil and cow manure we lug home from the Home Depot. The question is what to do with them. We develop strategies to combat them. With poison ivy we know special handling is required, likewise thistles, and anything with thorns has a built- in defense mechanism. We have fought back. We just about wiped out the bluebird and bald eagle population with our chemical warfare (DDT) that caused those birds to lay eggs with soft shells that couldn't withstand the mother's weight on the nest. Recently Round-up has been denounced for its carcinogenic properties for humans, all in the name of weed eradication, increasingly manicured landscapes or increased crop yields.

Whether in a garden or a church "weeds" present some unique opportunities for growth. Jesus offered words of caution about getting anxious and pulling the weeds before the wheat was ripe. (Traveling in the South one wonders if Jesus ever encountered kudzu vine!) Yet weeds aren't the only thing that just arrives in our garden or on our doorstep on Sunday morning. In churches there is often a congregational sigh of relief when a particularly thorny (aka demanding, offensive, odor-producing, clingy) congregant decides he/she have had enough and leaves. They had disrupted the flow of our well-ordered life, where there is a place for everyone, and everyone knows that place. Yet many pastors will tell you that when one leaves by the back door there is another walking through the front door simultaneously.

But part of creation's playful on-going surprise is wackiness. Being a Type A personality, I am a weed crusader. I bend, prune, lop, dig up or cover up offenders who pop up their heads up in my garden. I sense a particular failure if the offender gets to twelve inches without being seen by my all-knowing weed eye. I was particularly offended when a rather dry-leafed vagrant showed up in the bed of copperleaf, Thai ginger, and sweet almond. Its leaves were similar to the almond. I asked the landscaper and he didn't know. For some unexplained reason I decided to spare its life and wait and see what would happen. When we returned to Florida, I found the vagrant had an ephemeral circle of tiny white flowers growing right around the stem like a crown of fluff. It obviously wasn't an almond whose spiky white blossom grace the tips of the branches. I was still clueless.

Near our home is a nature trail between the front and back nines of a golf course. My eyes greedily took in all the new plant life on the trail and since the trail was new many of the species were marked. One of my loves were beauty berries whose tight rings of the most vibrant violet berries encircled the stems in concentric rings up the stem like puffs of smoke from the man on the billboard smoking Camels in Times Square eons ago. You guessed it, the volunteer in my garden was a beauty berry bush and because it volunteered in the middle of the tall copperleaf, I hadn't seen the flowers morphing into those vibrant violet berries I love. A weed, a volunteer, just think what I had almost whacked down! Jesus was right! Don't be in too big a hurry to get rid of the weeds. Our identification system is faulty. I could have lopped off something I love and never known it. It works in church too. Those who annoy us, trouble us, or ignore us have something to teach us. Mystics tell us in all creation everything belongs. To live in this changing and expanding world we need patience to wonder how it is we can live and learn and grow together. What do "the weeds" have to teach us? What of their worldview is instructive for understanding who we are as children of God? Like stones in a rock tumbler, our bumping and jostling each other can make us more useful to God and creation's purposes. Do

I have a gift from my worldview that might be helpful for someone else on his/her journey? In these dystopian times a watchful patience may be more growthful than divisive expulsions… and in some cases, far more beautiful.

BEST FRIENDS FOREVER

Texts: Acts 10:34-35, 44-48 and John 15:9-17

It was not too long ago that our granddaughters peppered their texts with a series of capital letters that signified important messages to those "in the know." Things like LOL-laughing out loud, TX for thanks, or BFF, best friends forever. Their world changes rapidly and they are now into emojis. One granddaughter even has an emoji that look like her that she can give them various facial expressions. Time moves quickly when you are teenager with the world in your hand; the challenge for this grandmother is to keep up.

In 2010 Philip Gulley, a Quaker minister, wrote the book, *If the Church Were Christian: Rediscovering the Values of Jesus.* For ten chapters Gulley explores ten areas where he believes the church needs to explore alternative theological constructs to be faithful to what Jesus taught about our life together. He gets right to the point in the first chapter, "If the Church Were Christian Jesus Would be a Model for Living Rather Than an Object of Worship."[63] With humor and grace, he tells about his surprise when he discovered that a teenaged friend was praying for him and Philip's church because the friend belonged to another denomination which held the vaunted opinion that his denomination was the true church, tracing

[63] Philip Gulley, If the Church Were Christian (NY: HarperCollins, 2010). Gulley's ten chapters chronicle the issues that divide the church today: affirming potential or condemning human sinfulness, reconciliation or judgment, right belief vs. the grace of God, questioning and imagining or having the answers, personal exploration vs. communal conformity, meeting needs vs. maintaining institutions, power or love, love or sexual control, this life or an afterlife.

their lineage directly to Jesus and were obedient to God's word. They were uniquely pure and untainted by the world. This was shocking because Philip had learned the same thing in his church! His friend had more resolve and within a year, Philip had joined his friend's church.

As an adult Philip reflected on the claim of ecclesiastical purity of any one church. We can't actually know what Jesus intended, the author contends. Regardless of whether we base our claim on apostolic succession, a literal reading of the inerrant Bible, or insight in spiritual revelation, Jesus said little about the incipient church.

Church Building 101

It would be fair to claim that Paul and other followers were much more intentional in church building than Jesus. At least they created a structure as the church grew and they assessed needs of the community. Jesus did, however, avoid fund raising, a huge time-consumer of many churches. Perhaps Jesus was confident that the Holy Spirit would guide and grow the church. The best guess is that Jesus never intended to found a church, although 39,000 Christian denominations, each with a slightly different take on the priorities of Jesus, think Jesus intended the church to look just like them.[64]

Philip Gulley was reared in the faith by his Catholic mother. His Baptist father was indifferent to his religious upbringing. Imagine when he left the church that taught him of the divinity, the purity, miracles, sinless of Jesus to become a Quaker there was a theological ocean for him to cross. The shore that Gulley arrived at was one where Jesus was no longer worshipped for his divinity but as a model of life rooted in his faith as a Jewish teacher, whose lifetime priorities were the care for the marginalized and the poor.

Two thousand years later and the struggle for the "one, true faith" continues. We've had councils that voted on nature of Jesus Christ, we've weeded out heretical beliefs and affirmed the Holy Spirit in the Western

---

64 ________, 4.

Church, as proceeding from God the Father and Jesus Christ the Son. But the Western Church still struggles to find a one-size-fits-all church. We laugh at the concern over how many angels could dance on the head of a pin debate of early church debates. Still the struggle continues to get church "right."

Enter Peter in today's lesson from Acts. Not only is he violating the holiness codes of Judaism, he's going to the top, a Roman centurion, a gentile who is considered ritually unclean to illustrate how this love of God that Jesus taught works. Previously Peter has had a puzzling dream. In it a large sheet full of all kinds of unclean animals came down and a voice told Peter to eat. The voice said, "What God has made clean, you must not call profane" (Acts 10:15 NRSV).

"Peter understands his dream and fairly explodes with his good news: 'It's God's own truth, nothing could be plainer: God plays no favorites! It makes no difference who you are or where you're from—if you want God and are ready to do as he says, the door is open. The Message he sent to the children of Israel—that through Jesus Christ everything is being put together again—well, he's doing it everywhere, among everyone'" (Acts 10: 34-36, *MSG*).

"No sooner were these words out of Peter's mouth than the Holy Spirit came on the listeners. The believing Jews who had come with Peter couldn't believe it either, the gift of the Holy Spirit was poured out on "outsider" Gentiles, but there it was—they heard them speaking in tongues, heard them praising God" (Acts 10: 44-46). Cornelius' household was full of the Holy Spirit. Peter commands them to be baptized. Of course, Peter got called to the home office, Jerusalem, to explain what he had been doing baptizing Gentiles.

Friendship with God

But that was what Jesus was about, too. He wanted his disciples to be included in that love he had experienced with God. He wanted them to know how to get there, what it felt like, to be filled with love that calms us with confidence, and makes us, like Peter willing to step outside the box to include others. Jesus offers us the true opportunity to BFF. It is not replaceable with an emoji, no matter how good the graphics.

Listen to Jesus' words: " I do not call you servants any longer, because the servant does not know what the master is doing; but I have called you friends, because I have made known to you everything that I have heard from my Father. You did not choose me, but I chose you. And I appointed you to go and bear fruit, fruit that will last, so that the Father will give you whatever you ask him in my name. I am giving you these commands so that you may love one another" (John 15: 15-17 NRSV).

It is friendship that we talk about every day, the kind takes care and nurture to grow. Jesus is an example, a model for us of friendship. If Philip Gulley is correct, Jesus is explaining how to be a good friend, developing the precious pieces of who we are, the way we are tied together, and God as the teacher and model of friendship.

The Gold of Our Lives

My mother spent her last days in the same extended care facility as her sister. Aunt Alice had lived there for three years when Mother moved it. The move was difficult for my mother, mainly, I think, because she liked to be in charge, and clearly this wasn't the place for Type A woman. She expressed her concerns to sister.

My aunt gave her the key to success in her new home. "Esther," my aunt began, "today learn the names of your nurses. Tomorrow call them by name every time they come into the room. The next day ask the names of their children and learn a little about them. The fourth day ask them how their children are, you know, like, 'how is John doing in the marching band?' On the fifth day you will have them eating out of the palm of your hand."

You may have had an experience like that. Someone beloved tries to give you a distillation of their life's lessons. Out of their deep love for you, they share what they believe is the gold of their life. They are leaving you their legacy of friendship.

Listening to Our Friend

Jesus is at the end of his life too. Our gospel lesson is taken from the rich section of John called the Farewell Discourses (John 13:1-17:26.) where Jesus is preparing his disciples for how they will live when Jesus is no longer physically with them. He is giving them the gold of his life, the secret of friendship.

If Philip Gulley is correct then Jesus is a model of living rather than an object of worship, we as disciples should be gathering close to Jesus to take in and savor each word Jesus uses to share how he and God live in deep friendship. A model of *friendship for us.* Not only was it important for first-century disciples but critical for us, who experience life in sound bites and a few words in a text. What does it take to live in that mutual relationship and mutual respect?

Notice Jesus doesn't begin with friends as problems to be solved but fellow travelers through life where what we do is to create the realm of God. In this kingdom friendship is based on obedience. Friendship begins with God's commandment to love one another. Sounds easy but we know that in our fractious society we are all about removing the speck from the other's eye before they can see well enough to come after the log in ours. We have lost the holy dimension of others: they are obstacles in our way, enemies to be cut down to size, representative of ideas or power that interfere with our closely held beliefs and doctrines. Jesus says friendship and obedience make our joy complete. The obedience isn't to an annotated list of dos and don'ts. It is to respect and love enemies, those who tricked or humiliated us, those who treated us spitefully. The trick is to let this command from God to love takeover our life.

Is Jesus Modelling Church Building?

Let's supposed Phillip Gulley is wrong. Let's suppose Jesus was giving very explicit directions on how to be the church. We heard them in our gospel reading: If you love me, obey my commandments. My joy will be in you and your joy complete. I have called you friends, you are no longer servants.

Barbara Brown Taylor, an Episcopalian priest in Northeast Georgia, was struggling with a call to the priesthood that chafed her spirit like a too-tight clerical collar chafes the neck. Maybe Jesus was talking about building the church, but it wasn't the institutional construct where hierarchy, ritual and formalized structure preceded the "two or three" who would gather to be open to each other following God's commandments to love extravagantly . A premier American preacher, Barbara Brown Taylor, decided finally hang up her clerical collar as a priest, a role that felt constricting. She decided to leave pastoral ministry and went on to teach World Religions at Piedmont College in rural Georgia. She explored the Spirit's promptings. She left that role to walk in friendship.

She tells of preparing for her first class. Her training as a priest prepared to get things right, but as the students stumbled in to an 8 a.m. class blurry eyed. Nothing she said resonated with them. She recalled why she had left the church. She decided to risk it all.

> She told the class, "With any luck," she wrote, "they were going to be saddled with questions that would keep them awake at night, increase both their awe before the mystery of life and their kinship with other mortals. I hoped that they would like my class. I told them, but that was not my main concern. My main concern was their utter transformation. I wanted their education to change their lives, their dreams, and their futures. I wanted what they learned to call all their old certainties into question and enlarge the boundaries of their known worlds. I wanted them to discover how capable they were, how rich their

> imaginations were, and how much their choices mattered in the grand scheme of things."[65]

Peter officiated at the baptism of Gentiles, in a Gentile home, and all those there were filled with joy! Jesus explains to his disciples that with God there aren't two columns, follower or friend. He has shared with them everything he learned from God, that's friendship. And we are called to respond to that friendship, forging our pathway as Christians have been doing since Jesus walked with his friends centuries ago. We are best friends who live with God's command to love one another as the emoji of the heart!

---

[65] Barbara Brown Taylor, *Leaving Church* (NY: HarperCollins, 2006) 208.

NORTHERN GARDENER

Garden Math

My mother loved to garden. Back in the 40's and 50's the preparation for a new growing season was the Burpee Seed Catalog. Arriving in the dead of winter my mother would pore over it like a rabbi reading Torah in the synagogue. She would discuss whether to buy the old favorite vegetables and flowers or to take a chance on a new variety that year. She never considered going to a nursery to buy anything other than a fruit tree. There just wasn't enough money to buy plants that were "Proven Winners" blooming in their six-inch pots with just the right blend of fertilizer, perlite and mulch to make instantly beautiful gardens after the last frost of spring.

My mother had a beautiful garden. There was the seven-sister rose in its variegated shades of pink. There were wild white roses with a fragrance that would make a bee swoon. June brought painted daisies. Delicate blue iris with their sword stems, peonies white, pink and red blossoms cascading to the ground with their heavy heads filled in every square inch of garden floor. Spirea with its white lacy sleeves dipped and swayed in the early summer breeze. My mother did not want in her garden. She was always getting something new to delight the eye, or enliven the fragrance of an early morning walk, beckoning both human and bird.

A farmer's wife has worries of crops, cattle, taxes, kids, but she gets good at God's math. How did she do it? Simple. She and the farm and town women in upstate New York practiced God's garden math. When a plant multiplied, they would dig it up and divide the abundance. She'd take a bucket or two of her new wealth the next time she went to church or a meeting. Some of those products of God's multiplication would be divided for one of my aunts in a neighboring town in exchange for some excess from her sister's garden. While they were subtracted from my mother's garden, they would add beauty to a new location, and created a space to fully enjoy another plant or to create a little openness in my mother's garden. Open space is needed to give dimension in a garden.

Our life in church is another example of God's math. We add richness to each other's life by sharing in this beloved community of faith. Sharing our gratitude, adding to each other's joy and carrying the burden with others, adds texture and beauty. Our caring and adding to the life of the community multiplies exponentially the joy and peace available and divides loneliness and sorrow into a size that may be assimilated or managed. Our participation in this healing and mysterious process increases our own compassion quotient. I often think that while our purpose in coming to church may be to get our batteries recharged for another week, God's purpose might be for us to be a pop of color in someone else's garden with a smile, being open to another, or listening or affirming others. Together we build up the body of Christ everywhere. Our blooms may be as fragrant as a gardenia blooming in the moonlight or an ancient lilac in the May sunshine. We may be as colorful and pungent as geraniums or marigolds. It is the new math of open hearts and grateful lives.

TACTILE TENDERNESS

We are getting settled! Slowly the moving boxes piled high in the den are lugged elsewhere to disgorge their contents in a permanent location. Yesterday I tugged the dish box to the glass fronted cabinets in the kitchen. I was able to fit nine of the twelve wine, water, and cordial glasses into the cabinet where they sparkled in the overhead lights. When I opened the box, I discovered that I had wrapped them in the various colored tissue paper from the basement in our former home. So, when I peeled back the tape from the box there was a cacophony of colors protecting the glasses, pink and turquoise, lime and black, forest and sunshine, and some in plain Jane white. Releasing the glasses from the wrinkled paper, a mosaic of joy grew at my feet. I was delighted!

I had forgotten I had used up the colored tissue paper to wrap the crystal. Color cascading and light coruscating on crystal and glass shelves. My recycling spirit bloomed when the remaining glasses that did not fit on the shelves nestled in the colored tissue in a box that just fit on the top shelf over the refrigerator. It was like touching holy objects in a dark paneled church swathed in rich silk paraments. They were ensconced in their new home and I was softened up for sacred in surprising venues, like our kitchen.

The next delight was anticipated. We had ordered two big bookcases, bought an extra shelf for each to hold my tons of books that I had to have in our new home. Gordon and Jeremiah delivered them in a Tuesday Florida downpour, bolted them together for stability. They put them directly opposite the windows, all seven feet tall by six feet wide in our bedroom. Unpacking those twelve boxes of bankers' boxes was wrapping myself in joy. A shelf for the Nouwen books, gathering all the Brueggemann books, Borg and Crossan books on the same shelf, side-by-side where they will always be after our Borg-Crossan trip to Turkey in 2011. Next came the books of poetry, Biblical reference books, and psychology and theology. Just unpacking them, knowing they were accessible once again and in even better order then when I had taken them off the basement bookshelves in Illinois was a joy. I don't love the books per se but the minds and ideas of the authors who have given their lives to wonder, explore and explain through the lens of their experience their purview of existence, that excites me. When I am lost, angry, afraid, stymied I can go to the shelves and invite one of them to show me a better world than where I am currently ensnared, a more generous horizon, or a calming sense of proportion. Just touching and arranging those books brings me to a better place, a holy habitation of other restless souls, who with Augustine are looking to rest their restless souls in Thee. Twelve empty cartons later, many friends standing with their backs to me, straight and tall, I felt settled for the first time since we had moved.

Our bed is beneath the window, directly opposite the bookcase. Books shelved, my husband and I took a nap, a wonderful pleasure of retirement. I prayed aloud, "Now I lay me down to sleep/My beloved books at my feet." My senses heightened, full of two days of tactile tenderness, more fully alive, we snoozed, content and preparing for the joy in the morning in the next chapter of our lives.

NORTHERN GARDENER

Advent Landscapes

Marcus Tullius Cicero said, "If you have a garden and a library, you have everything you need." Gardeners know that they need the soil with which to play and God's words in which they can take root. During Advent we wait and watch, reflect and prepare for the birth of peace in our heart. There are four weeks before Christmas to examine our animosities and hatreds, to practice the discipline of prayer and meditation, and to look within to see how each of us can become a birthing room for commitment and hope. Advent landscapes are places to watch, to be quiet and focus our attention on what these places can teach us. Isaiah, Matthew, and Luke are rich resources for our Advent library, if you will, to give insight, to prepare the soil for the wolf and the lamb to eat together, where no one hurts or destroys on God's holy land.

So much of the time we are trying to differentiate ourselves from others. We create boundaries that say you are only good if you embrace my/our beliefs. But suppose God is taking us all through this Advent landscape so we can peek over the stout walls that separate us to see that the Creator God has created all things for us richly to enjoy. Our task is not to create gridlock but an openness, so together, with all our foibles, brokenness and grudges, we limp into Bethlehem to see God's great gift to us all, a vulnerable, tiny one, who with our nurture, can live and learn and grow with us, grow in us, into full stature.

John O'Donohue says in *Walking in Wonder*, "Landscape is an incredible mystical teacher, and when you begin to tune into its sacred presence something shifts inside you."[66] When we begin to see ourselves in the Advent landscape, we gain a new sense of who we are. We are the precious and unique creation of God, but we are also a part of a much larger thing: we are all woven into the sustainable web of life whose purposes are greater than we might otherwise imagine and more healing than the scars writ large on so many lonely lives.

Prisoners in southern Illinois were learning gardening skills and planting their own gardens. They learned an employable skill, something they may not have had before, and they could see first-hand how they are an integral part of the web of life. One story from a United Church of Christ publication tells of a prisoner released from prison who called back to the prison to ask how his eggplants were doing. He had planted the seeds in tiny peat pots in the greenhouse, transplanted them, nurtured and fertilized them and they were now ready to be put in the soil of God's garden. The Advent landscape had taught this young man a mystical lesson; something inside him cared deeply. Wouldn't it be wonderful if we could see our Advent landscape as mystical moving us closer to that Holy Ground? Here a humble Prince tends gardens of hope and harvests food for the world's hungry and instead of saying "Merry Christmas," we would ask, "How are your eggplants growing?"

[66] John O'Donohue, *Walking in Wonder* (NY: Convergent Books, 2015) 24.

HAROLD RAMIS DIED...NO KIDDING

Harold Ramis died Monday, February 2, 2014. His *Miami Herald* obituary said Mr. Ramis "died peacefully surrounded by family and friends."[67] At the Academy Awards the following Sunday his name was listed in a memorial tribute to those who died in the film industry in the past year.

Harold Ramis was Bill Murray's bespectacled sidekick in *Ghostbusters.* Starting in Second City Harold Ramis cavorted through *National Lampoon's Animal House, Caddyshack,* and *Groundhog Day.* But Harold Ramis died, no kidding. Dan Aykroyd called his friend "a generous, nurturing, humble guy." He was saddened by the loss of (his) brilliant, gifted, and funny friend. "May he now get the answer he was always seeking."[68]

What was Harold Ramis seeking? We are told comedians often have a manic quality that tosses them like a tennis ball in a game between a novice and a pro. Stingingly accurate shots and then faltering returns into the net. Nadia Bolz-Weber describes the comedic roller-coaster ride in her book, *Pastrix.* She tells of one of her comedic friends who "was like one of those cloth dolls with long skirt that you turn upside down and pull the skirt up---and it's no longer granny, but the big bad wolf. The right side-side-up doll is the fun-loving and charismatic host, flipped over, a non-functioning depressive."[69]

---

[67] Ramis Obituary, *The Miami Herald,* February 25, 2014, B4.

[68] https://dailymail.co.uk/tvsshowbiz/article-2567355/Bill-Murray-leads-tributes-Ghostbusters-star-Harold-Ramis-dies-age-69.html

[69] Nadia Bolz-Weber, *Pastrix* (NY: Jericho Books, kindle ed. 2013).

Harold Ramis' comedy "always had a nuanced meaning, an almost Buddhist philosophy," said Andrew Alexander, president and CEO of The Second City.[70] In Ramis' classic *Groundhog Day* Bill Murray stars in the story of a man who relives the same day over and over as he examines his life. How was it that Harold Ramis could find in the craziness, weirdness, disappointment, and out-of-control feelings that assault our day-to-day experience the nuanced meaning in life?

The same week that Ramis died the *Miami Herald* told of the work of a music therapist, Joe Goelz, at Seasons Hospice as he gave his musical, spiritual guidance to an elderly woman who was dying. Joe Goelz helped his client complete the tasks experts say are important to closing out our relationships here on earth: I love you. I forgive you. Please forgive me. Thank you and goodbye. With his guitar, Joe strummed, sang, and helped one woman to complete her end-of-life tasks.[71] Did Harold Ramis see the tasks of living well as the same as dying well? Googling Harold Ramis you will find that *Groundhog Day* became a point of profound divergence with Bill Murray, the star of that movie. A rift that lasted twenty years. But does living well mean we are seeking ways to say and hear--- forgiveness, both the given and the received, a word of thanks and love and acknowledgement of our existence?

I remember being really annoyed at a religious tract someone had handed me long ago. It advocated living every day as if it is your last. What kind of nonsense is this to tiptoe through your life waiting and looking over your shoulder for the Grim Reaper to lockstep with you? I resented the life requirement to be the first to say the word of peace, acceptance or praise when others traipsed over my feelings like pansies planted too close to the edge of the sidewalk. It seemed like an angry God threatening me with a really big stick if I didn't "play nice." My response was couched in angry terms. But did I need to take a step back and see the huge abyss created when the playing field has been destroyed with broken relationships creating

---

[70] https://www.yahoo.com/entertainment/news-39-writer-actor-harold-ramis-dies-191127540.html

[71] Patricia Burns, "Music Therapy Enhances Hospice Patients' Quality of Life" *The Miami Herald,* February 24, 2014, A1.

crevasses and debris all over it? What's it like for people who are keenly aware that they are playing on a lop-sided field? Harold Ramis is dead, no kidding.

Dan Aykroyd said Harold was looking for something all his life. His rift with Bill Murray over Groundhog Day came at a time when their intense creative disagreements were exacerbated by Murray's personal difficulties. Twenty years later, when Ramis was dying, a donut-laden Bill Murray showed up at Ramis' house complete with a 7 a.m. police escort. Ramis had great difficulty speaking by that time, but he listened and reminisced with Murray. Joe Goelz's instructions probably weren't spoken. But with donuts and his police escort the two estranged men parted as friends. A relationship repaired, Murray gave a touching tribute to Ramis at the Academy Awards. And a twenty-year-old breach was healed.[72]

Author Pat Conroy's life was so traumatized by his brutal Marine father and his Southern belle wannabe mother that he and his siblings lived in terror much of their growing up. Conroy's South Carolina childhood and college years were the grist for many of his novels. Yet he and his father made peace by sharing a love of cooking, particularly chili. They never got to the kind of farewell that Goelz employs but they participated in bridge building connecting continents too long apart.

There is a Lenten hymn that asks, "What language shall I borrow to thank thee, dearest friend?" For Bill Murray and Harold Ramis and Pat Conroy and his father it was the language of food. Food, the great community builder. How wonderful it is to check out giving those who have walked with us a peace-building farewell, the kind Joe Goelz helps his clients experience. It can make the future seem more bearable for those left behind. My hunch is a lot of folks never get those Hallmark moment farewells. They are left rummaging through their book of memories looking for those words of peace hidden in another language. But that iconic movie, "Groundhog Day" offers us hope: we often can replay some scenes until we find the answer we have been seeking.

---

72 https://www.amazon.com/Ghostbusters-Daughter-Life-Harold-Ramis/dp/0735217874/ref=sr_1_1?dchild=1&keywords=ghostbusters+daughter&qid=1617472991...

NORTHERN GARDENER

Trolls in the Forest, Gnomes in the Garden

The Morton Arboretum is a 1,700-acre home for trees from all over the world. Build by Joy Morton, founder of Morton Salt, and located in Lisle, Illinois, a recent woodland delight came as trolls who are the "protectors of the forest" descended on the arboretum. These woodland creatures are tucked behind trees and were made of recycled wood from a lumber yard and trees that had been cut down on the property. These whimsical creatures are poised to catch unsuspecting folks who venture into their domain. They have the best interests of the trees at heart. Catching a wandering child or throwing boulders at cars as they enter the parking lot are part of their duties.

My husband and I got together with the trolls twice. It was such a delight. Maps help kids search for clues to the trolls' treasure. One clue is at each troll. But what has been so much fun to watch is the parents and grandparents who are given permission to be kids themselves. One exhibit is a troll with a cage-like trap, ready to lure stray children into his lair. The trolls' expressions---menacing, quizzical, slightly sinister, full of delight---suck us into the world where things aren't taken too seriously. Playful trolls lure us into fantasy.

Gnomes inhabit the world on a smaller scale. Many people tuck a few gnomes in shady corners of their gardens to keep the spirit world of the garden running smoothly. With their pointy hats they watch for the fairies and other mythical creatures who call the garden home. Gnomes watch stock-still, pulling themselves up to their full height of twelve or fifteen inches, to reign over their green domain. Perhaps you have met a few in the gardens you frequent. They offer the invitation to let your imagination take you to a slower world with time for wondering and wandering, mischief and mystery, remembering and developing a healthy appetite for the surprises, joy and laughter of playful children. Being God's child is a lifelong assignment. It's incredibly enjoyable to do our homework in the forests and gardens of our lives. But watch out in the forest and garden!

NORTHERNER GARDENER

Vest Pocket Gardens

Gardens do not have to be big to be beautiful. I noticed that in New Orleans. There, well cared-for gardens bring joy even among the ancient buildings. Some can be glimpsed through wrought-iron gates. Others treat when you walk deep inside a building and spy a vest-pocket size garden through a door to a courtyard. New Orleans gardens have a charm all their own. There are rules for those gardens that do not get sunshine all day. Plants must be chosen to accommodate less light. Rainfall must be taken into account. Properly planted and cared for, vest pocket gardens can delight the eye. When they are not cared for, they bring a little jolt of sadness or nostalgia.

Our lives are in God's garden. How we tend our lives can bring joy to God's heart. Caring for our bodies, our spirits, our prayer life and in turn being sensitive and concerned for others is growthful. Committing the time needed to spend in quiet, in reading, reflecting, and praying enriches the soil. Noxious weeds need to be closely watched but not necessarily pulled out thus endangering the "the good stuff."

Gardens reveal new gardens. A couple of weeks ago I decided to move a large cinnamon fern to the front of our house and put it in front of a trellis. To do this I had to move the existing peace lily around to the back. When I transferred the lily out back, I noticed that the roots were just a tangle. With careful tugging and pulling Alan and I were to separate one lily into five. I transplanted three and potted two of the new-found "lily children to give to someone who might be looking for a little peace in their life and have a shady spot to grow them.

Vest pocket gardens are tiny moments tucked away from the glaring lights of the busy world. No media or social media measure their significance; no big board indexes their going up or coming down. Yet they can exert great force, not by spectacular pronouncements, or sagacious plans for saving something, but by discipline and steadfastness in blooming where they are planted, ignored in the hustle, bustle and self-importance of "real life." The surprise of their witness in our hearts is often noted as an afterthought. Oh, so that's what she meant? He just did it, all those years without saying a word! Vest pocket gardens are often recognized in hindsight. The Israelites only got to see the back of God as he passed over. But the warmth of God's presence like vest pocket gardens remains after having turned many corners.

Most of us are vest-pocket size. Yet we are tended and cared for by the gardener who threw the planets around the sun, got them spinning, and makes the rain to fall on the just and unjust. We have great potential to bloom in our unique way as the frangipani does in the church garden---from seemingly dead branches come the gentlest fawn-colored blossoms and softest fragrance, reminding us that new life emerges in tiny, unexpected places. In tending our tiny plots carefully, God is pleased.

THE RIVER FLOWS

There's an old tree where the river bends
Gnarled, torn, broken and forlorn
Tree watched all the water roll
Tree swayed, bent in the windy toll.

Chorus:
The river flows by my path
The river flows, I sometimes laugh
The river flows, it's changing just like me
Come join hands with the restless sea.

Dangle my feet in that cool stream
Like a kid: fishing pole and dreams
Sitting there clouds a-playing tag
Life is carefree, no spirits sag.

Don't have success to hear folks talk
But they haven't seen what's here
The spider's web is laced with dew
Each morning creation plays anew.

We've seen the seasons come and go
Made white-winged angels in the snow
We've moved to the rhythm, we've watched the flow
Thank God your speed for us is slow.

Hymn Tune: Jim Strathdee, *Light of the World*

IS EASTER A NOUN OR A VERB?

Texts: John 20:19-23 and Acts 6:1-7

At Easter each of us is asked how we keep and incorporate that familiar and difficult story of Easter for our spiritual toolkit. John's gospel tells us Jesus gives us the peace of the Holy Spirit after all the horror of the crucifixion. That peace, that Holy Spirit, will be so good we will have to share it. Jesus' blessing is ours on this first Sunday of Eastertide, or Whit Sunday. Growing up in the Methodist church we always called the Sunday after Easter Low Sunday. I thought "low" referred to the attendance that day after the glory and beauty of the Easter service. I later learned that this Sunday is called Whit Sunday or low Sunday was because those newly baptized members of the early church during the Great Easter Vigil were given white robes to wear after their baptism. Those robes were emblems of their new life proudly worn the first week after their early Easter morning baptism. Now a week later they had to return to their everyday clothes. But something was different. In the gift of baptism, the Holy Spirit had been poured out upon them as surely as the water washed their bodies.

On Easter Sunday, my husband and I worshiped at our church in Florida. The pastor told of two caterpillars who were contentedly eating milkweed leaves and growing quite large. They looked up and saw a graceful butterfly floating in the breeze. One looked at the other and said, "They'll never get me up in one of those contraptions." But one first Sunday after Easter we are up in one of those contraptions. It seems that no matter our emotions and feelings, our pains, regrets, and bruising during Holy Week, we are in one of those contraptions. We are Easter people, given the freedom to move ur hearts as butterflies move their wings. Given the Spirit to offer others the same: to become beautiful like a butterfly, to move to other gardens, to change toxic environments, and to behold the vastness of creation and how we might all live peaceably in God's garden right here and right now.

My Easter Story

Easter stories make me a little edgy. I'm not sure I have grasped God's great truth of Easter. And I am also suspicious that others may not have either. But this is my Easter story of how a new understanding of resurrection came at an Easter Sunrise service sitting on folding chairs in the wet grass before dawn. It had rained during the night which isn't unusual in Florida. The sun wasn't up and was I still groggy. The contemporary band in which our son plays bass guitar was doing a bluegrass service. We had told him we'd be there.

Bluegrass music created a new setting for me to envision the Easter story: sun breaking over the mountains into the hollows in Appalachia. Turning on the mics, the Plantation, Florida 9-to-5ers looked a little out of character in their plaid shirts, bandanas, and straw hats but they were getting into it. A fine banjo player from Miami joined the group that morning. There is no percussion in bluegrass, so the beat is carried in the bass. In the mountains it would have been a double bass. Here with palm trees in the background, the music cranked up. I could hear the deep resonating thunks of the bass undergirding this expression of the hill country's telling of the first Easter. Bluegrass roots have swept from the hill and heather of Scotland and the emerald fields of Ireland to a new home in the Appalachian Mountains and the Piedmont Plateau hills of Kentucky, West Virginia and the uplands of the Carolinas. My tennis shoes dew laden, I was bathed in a whole new depth of a bluegrass Easter story. A rhythm of life, filled with incredible hardship, agony, and treacherous paths as they had climbed dense underbrush and rocky hillsides, only to find what there was no welcome committee of town folk awaiting their arrival, but a lot of what they had left behind was here too. The bass marked that time. Yet rapidly plunking of those banjo fingers quickly found the *joie de vivre,* the dance of life in a new world, the bubbling joy, the joy of Jesus, had come wit them. The banjo's notes articulated their Easter experience. The fiddle created bridges between old and new realities, back and forth, back and forth. Together a new world, rooted in their history, celebrating the gift of today with lightness and hope.

A whole new meaning was rolled out for me in the dawn's early rays. It was so far from my accustomed take on Easter. This new expression brought to something that I had figured I was an expert in, being a minister and all. Just like beauty, isn't it? Born of unimagined pain only to worm its way into your heart with the sound like raindrops dancing on a tin roof or a baby's soft coo.

The tumbling, flowing, foot stomping music chipped away at my assumptions about Easter. Hearing with your heart and let it "sit a while," like two folks in rocking chairs on the porch, things start to shift. There are new responses. My notions began to rub up against the realities of others who experienced life and Easter vastly differently than I had. My middle-class assumptions were introduced to an embodied joy in response to what happened in Jerusalem 2000 years ago and had traveled many miles through many cultures and time. My stuffy attitudes encountered Easter joy and it pulled me by the hand into the dance of life. That may have been what was going on Easter morning. Is Easter a noun or a verb?

A Get-Going Easter Story

The two readings for this Whit Sunday create a container for us. We're to take off our white baptismal robes and get going on our faith journeys. In John's gospel the disciples are trying to assimilate Mary Magdalene's news of the abandoned tomb that morning after the catastrophic Holy Week. And now 12 hours later, in walks Jesus through the locked doors. They were trying to keep the religious authorities and Romans from arresting them. Even with their garrison mentality, Jesus broke down those constructs and says: ta-da---this is what I want you to do. Take the peace and power of the Holy Spirit and get going. Just as God sent me, I send you.

Their joy must have been boundless…until they remembered how they had acted in the past week. Whoa! The week was a catalog of denial, betrayal, running and hiding, failure to speak up for one falsely accused. In the light of Jesus' radiant face, they were condemned. But Eugene Peterson's *The Message*, John 20:22-23, has Jesus freeing the disciples, and us, from wallowing in our past and our shortcomings. The risen Christ tells the disciples what's he's been doing. Listen: "If you forgive someone's sins, they are gone for good. If you don't forgive sins, what are you going to do with them?"

It sounds like rhetorical question, but Jesus wants an answer. What are we going to do with all the things that we drag along behind us and haul out every time we need an excuse for not living as an Easter person? What *are* we going to do with them?

A Biblical Food Fight

The early Christian community has an answer for that question. In Acts they are living as Easter people and things are cooking. Folks are hungry for the word, and a multi-cultural community sprouted. But soon there are cracks in the new community. We know the litany --- those folks are not like us. We're not getting our fair share. Our widows are not getting as many food stamps as the widows who always lived on this street. The early apostles needed whistles to referee all the arguing and harangues. They saw the focus of the community shifting from God's amazing love on the cross to "me, my, mine." If they didn't respond quickly the momentum of the community would devolve into an ethnic food fight. They didn't like to sling hash. They would strike a blow for the Holy Spirit and creativity.

"How about getting some strong leaders in the community to take this food ministry on as their mission?" they ask. "We'll bet some have a knack for this. It's a way to move forward." Notice what they didn't do. They didn't say, "We never did it that way before." They didn't worry that there wouldn't be enough because so many were joining. They didn't show concern tha some followers in Jerusalem might be freeloaders, joining for the benef but they were adamant that everyone should contribute something.

Message, Acts 6:7, closes with this interesting summary. "The Word of God prospered. The number of disciples in Jerusalem increased dramatically. Not the least, a great many priests submitted themselves to the faith."

It says that? The priests and the ministers are joining. How did they sneak in? Have the scribes and Pharisees had a post-resurrection experience? Acts is telling us something we already know; faithful living is compelling. The practices of the early Christians, Jew and gentile alike, were being watched and found authentic by many including the priestly workers in Jerusalem. Faithful living attracts others. Those followers knew God provided a container large enough to hold the vast array of religious practices and beliefs in that ancient Near Eastern city and still hold the true center on God. Authentic living welcomes by the sheer force of its joy, just like bluegrass music from the hills. Easter living makes us credible; we are changed by God's action.

Is Easter a noun or a verb? Is Easter a noun, an event two millennia ago, complete with Roman soldiers and sneaky Pharisees? Or is it a verb that changes us, from the inside out? Is it God's action becoming our action that moves us to listen, to see, to gather and to forgive? I believe Easter is a verb full of life and action, capable of changing our frightened and hard hearts. Good news for a low Sunday.

NORTHERN GARDENER

Backdrop

On the Sunday we painted the Thrift Shop/Sunday School building; many hands worked diligently on our project. I was amazed when I walked into the garden after the sunny yellow color had been painted on the wall which had been a greyish-white concrete windowless end of a classroom. Having worked a lot in the garden I was familiar with the garden, yet that pop of sunshine created a vibrant backdrop for the flowers, shrubs, and trees. The plantings had new definition and clarity; each part shone in a new way and was happily integrated with the other parts into a relationship that made my heart sing.

Sometimes we feel like we are just a backdrop for the real stars. They do all the important stuff and get all the attention and we hang out in the background. In painting the wall, I realized there were no stars and supporting characters. A garden setting reveals each player critical in the grand design, the mosaic of life, all engaged in a creating community. Each part of a garden creates a totality greater than the sum of its parts. Our challenge and joy are to be the best for others so that our time together is pleasing to God for we are co-creating something much larger than ourselves.

When gifted education was a hot topic in public education, there was on voice that reminded us everyone has a gift. Paul Torrance helped educat to understand that all children have some area in their life where truly have a gift to share with the world. He encouraged teachers to at each child to discover giftedness within and encourage that gift. As in the garden, not every flower or bush is going to be in bloom all the time, and people will not ooh and aah over it constantly. Gardens, like lives, are an evolving work in progress. But each part contributes to the overall enjoyment of the garden.

Each of us is called to be a part—a blossom, the backdrop, a pot that fills in a dark corner, we all have a place, a part of God's supporting cast that creates beauty. Our call is also to be a viewer who lets the loveliness of God's diverse and colorful creation fill our soul and heart with prayers of gratitude. With this attitude adjustment, we see how God calls each of us to put down roots in this growing community!

HONESTLY

I never thought much about my soul or that it might be my longed-for destination, a funny statement for a pastor. Soul was just a nebulous term fraught with self-righteousness right up there with "God told me" and "my personal savior." Saving my soul smelled too much of a self-absorbed religiosity that knew exactly what God wanted and how to get it. Contrary to my roots, it felt like the Vietnam era T-shirt which said, "Kill 'em all and let God sort 'em out." Soul I had left as one of God's duties, being the judge and all. But as a pastor, I knew that my religious snobbery did not preclude me from struggling with soul in those terrains where reflection is inevitable. I also had the disquieting sense that this God of love who wooed me, just as he had wooed Jeremiah, would not abandon those whose ear could hear lament at a hundred paces. A wooing God would not abandon.

I went to another pastor's dinner discussion of soul at a bowling alley. What a gift that dinner was to me! I started giving serious consideration to the precious given of our existence that develops throughout life and moves beyond the limits of our moment on the human stage. Is there a collective nature of soul? Is soul the conduit through which we appropriate and contain our earthly experience?

Pen in hand I tried to get some handles on soul:
You ask me what is soul as you
pull your lawn chair round to
catch the day's last rays over
the grey-black lake.

It is you, it is I colorblind
to the tips of our toes as
orangey fingers are reeled into
raspberry heavens.

It is the lake standing
imperceptibly grander in
response to Moon's strong tug.

It is the Senecas dancing in fire
circles at the corn festival. It is,
my dears, a road to the totality
of air and water, wing and hoof, awakening
to find the Time Traveler has called
us all to twirl as the red-headed
girl in an ecstatic dance before
falling exhausted in a pile of
crunchy giggles.

Talk about what goes around coming around. I am going to have to get cozy, or at least acquainted with my soul. That is hardly what I had in mind as I struggle to get this book off the ground. But this book is to instruct me and not, as I previously thought, to imbue the world with my wisdom. I can only share my take, on what I am discovering. It will be laying bare of my life, and let you, "Gentle Reader," to use Miss Manners' nomenclature, decide what rings true for you. The vulnerability frightens me. Suppose that I cannot hop, skip and jump over the soul piece.

The ability to say things carefully has allowed me to say some disputatious stuff in the heartland pulpits I have served and get out relatively unscathed. My fear of offending is the guardian of my tongue. I have a complete set of tapes on file in my head to remind me of my *faux pas*. But I notice time is running out. My friends are completing their journeys and we are all on the same path.

e fear of being exposed as a phony, a faint copy of someone else's bright looms large. Indeed, all our ideas, I suspect, are ragged fragments from our imperfect gathering of others' thoughts pieced together in a coat of many colors to either warm us in our humanity or wrap us away, solitary and unused, fearing corruption, dilution, or absorption. In the ancient world writing in the school of your intellectual or spiritual mentor was an identifying mark. Oftentimes one wrote using their mentor's name. Today plagiarism has a network of legal ramifications. Acknowledging I am not the sharpest knife in the drawer, I still long to share the perceptions of others with my wild-eyed dreams and recycled notions. Still the defenses around my house of cards would make the ramparts around a medieval castle seem paltry. The tough mental work of refining ideas and then standing with them to see where they lead is a daunting task. As I peer over my glasses, I don't see the world needing my "fine touch." Instead I see myself as a creature asking the existential question: Is there more? How do I get to that mirrored lake where the Senecas dance and the giggling girl falls exhausted after the corn dance?

For soul may not be some ethereal notions floating around in my head but rather concretized action. Dietrich Bonhoeffer said, "[It is] not to do just anything, but to do what is right, and to dare; not to float about in the possible, but to bravely seize the real. Freedom is not the flight of thoughts, but only in action. Move out of anxious hesitation into the storm of events, borne only to God's commandment and your faith, and freedom will receive your spiritual exultation."[73]

Bonhoeffer's notion of receiving our spiritual wings when we risk, dare in the face of the storm, was put to the test as I nervously prepared to give a talk to the Friends of the Helen B. Hoffmann Library about my book, *Thanksgiving Leads to Christmas,* the next morning. I developed a strategy. I would share all the things I had learned along the publishing path. For instance, I had first imagined my book audience would be my family but it didn't speak to their condition at that stage of their lives. They were busy getting their kids launched, careers firmly established and were not ready for this trip down memory lane. I would tell of the costs financially and

[73] Dietrich Bonhoeffer, *Letters and Papers from Prison* (NY: Touchstone, 1953) 184. Quoted in Richard Rohr and Andreas Ebert, *The Enneagram*, (NY: Crossroad Publishing, 2016) 130.

emotionally and my frustration of being shipped from one department to another at the publisher, from one assistant to another, as the manuscript was moved from desk to desk. Only questions germane to their tiny fiefdom could be answered.

Between sips of coffee and bites of date bread the Friends were right with me. They laughed with me at all the times I fell flat on my face during the process, particularly after working for two months selecting the color pictures to accompany each story, the publisher sent back the galley proofs in black and white. Mine was not a shining result as much as blind luck and serendipity as one could imagine without asking the Holy Spirit to stand up and take a bow.

But holding your first box of books from the publisher, I told them, is like when the nurse puts your firstborn in your arms. There are no words. Washing over me were so many emotions it was impossible to untangle them had I wanted to, for despite imperfections, faults, and failings I was overcome with the magnitude of what I was holding in my hand. Surely, I had not been on this process alone.

I related how the title of that book, *Thanksgiving Leads to Christmas,* made my relationship with my husband go more smoothly for I am reminded at various levels of my being that thanking him and appreciating the things he does for me has made our relationship more joy filled. But what became apparent in that book talk was how receptive the women were who listened. They could have gone on leading their amazing lives without me, but what *I* needed was their receiving me so warmly. The truth of the matter was when the layers of varnish, fear, and self-loathing were stripped away I stood in the circle of humanity where others helped me in my process, which is reason enough to put myself out there in the first place. When I pray with my spiritual director, she always puts both hands forward, one hand up and one hand down, one hand to give, one hand to receive. That date bread Monday brought the two hands forward, for giving *and receiving*: "For in giving, we receive," goes the prayer attributed to St. Francis of Assisi. For it is here we come to that field where the place so full that our souls overflow and we do not need to speak of it.

On September 14, 2001, three days after 9/11, film critic Roger Ebert wrote a column entitled "Make It Green."

> If there is to be a memorial, let it not be of stone and steel. Fly no flag above it, for it is not the possession of a nation but a sorrow shared with the world.
>
> Let it be a green field, with trees and flowers. Let there be paths that wind through the shade.
> Put out park benches where old people can sun in the summertime, and a pond where children can skate in the winter.
>
> Beneath this field will lie entombed forever some of the victims of September 11.
> It is not where they thought to end their lives. Like the sailors of the battleship Arizona, they rest where they fell.
>
> Let this field stretch from one end of the destruction to the other. Let this open space among the towers mark the emptiness in our hearts. But do not think of it a sad place.
> Give it no name.
> Let people think of it as the green field.
> Every living thing that is planted there will show faith in the future.
>
> Let students take a corner of the field and plant a crop there. Perhaps corn, our native grain.
> Let the harvest be shared all over the world, with friends and enemies, because that is the teaching of our religions, and we must show that we practice them.
> Let the harvest show that life prevails over death, and let the gifts show that we love our neighbors.

Do not build again on this place. No building can stand there.
No building, no statue, no column, no arch, no symbol, no name, no date, no statement.
Just the comfort of the earth we share, to remind us that we share it.[74]

Here I found my soul. In the comfort of the earth we share and the reminder that we share it.

ttps://www.rogerebert.com/roger-ebert/ten-things-i-know-about-the-mosque
t 19, 2010.

COME NOW MY CHILDREN

Come now, my children, come now my children
Professing the love you share.
You've been nurtured from birth with laughter and mirth
Now receive this blessing with care.
Come now, my children, come now my children
Come to the Presence your family and friends are here
Together we pray the joy of this day
Will grow through each act and year.

Here now, my children, in this moment
A mystery is revealed.
Love lights a flame and trusting you claim,
That together with God you'll go
Who in this moment can imagine how your young lives will unfold?
Through joy and through pain, through sunshine and rain
Keep those promises so bold.

Go now, my children, with feasting and dancing
We witnessed the power we praise.
For God sets the table and Christ pours the wine
And the Spirit sets you free.
Go now, my children, strengthened for serving
God, neighbor, friend and foe
This grace will enfold you, so open your arms
That God's light through you will glow.
Hymn Tune: Share the Spirit, IRR.
For Weddings, Confirmation.

CONNECT THE DOTS!

Out beyond ideas of wrongdoing and rightdoing,
there is a field. I'll meet you there.
...Rumi, 13th century Sufi mystic, Islamic scholar and poet

Flying home from Palestine in June 2014 I knew the title of my next book...*Better Than Right*. For it was in Palestine that I first encountered the Sufi mystic's quote which captured the immensity of what I would struggle years to articulate. Not that I wanted to write a book, mind you. I had written one in 2013 and it was grueling. Yet *Better Than Right* was swirling around in my head. Getting back home I had tried to write about my experiences there. Front and center were the three refugee camps, Aida, Jenin, and Ramallah, that our Episcopalian women's group had visited. Two of us, Caroline Cracraft and I had visited a fourth camp, Shuafat in East Jerusalem. Those refugee camp images were seared in my mind.

The inception of the refugee question began in November 1917 when the Western powers were deciding what to do about the Jewish question in Europe. Specifically, British Foreign Secretary Arthur James Balfour wrote a letter to Lionel Walter, a leader of the Jewish Community in Britain conveying first political recognition by a great power that Palestine might be a national home for Jewish people and, secondly "nothing shall be done which may prejudice the civil and religious rights of existing non-Jewish communities in Palestine." The first provision, recognizing Zionism, has been accomplished at a huge cost, and the second has been trampled and ignored. What the Palestinian refugees had endured, are enduring, seems eternal. Yet their creativity and steadfast persistence in the face of ever-increasing and crushing confinement can only amaze.

My History Lesson

Everyone always prefaces their remarks about Israel with, "It is a complex situation." My first memory of the Palestinian situation was when I was 8 or 9 hearing on the radio of the fighting between the Palestinian fighters and Israeli patriots. There was no shadow of doubt---the Palestinians were the aggressor. The Israelis were just seeking a homeland after the brutality of the Holocaust. With the United Nations supporting their endeavor, they were creating a state for the Jews. That mindset was reinforced as the news reported Israel's attempts to establish themselves throughout Palestine, establish kibbutzes where the desert could bloom with justice. The wars that pushed the Palestinians into refugee camps in Jordan, Lebanon, and Syria, and within Israel were an unmentioned part of the price.

The crack in the bell that let a little light in for me was in the early 90s when a retiring conference minister in the Illinois Conference of the United Church of Christ took an interim assignment in Turkey helping the stream of Palestinian refugees searching for a homeland. The backlog and logjam that these homeless persons, both Muslim and Christian, faced as they tried to emigrate to life free of persecution seemed insurmountable. Those Christian relief workers worked tirelessly on resettlement and remained steadfast in applying pressure on those slowly grinding gears for hope, dignity, decency, humanity, and a place to call home.

That trip to Palestine was a life changer in what I didn't know how to articulate. I did no church talks when I came home. I was careful not to offend my Jewish friends nor my many friends who found the Palestinian question a betrayal of a commitment to American ideals. I did write a long letter to the editor to the *Chicago Tribune* but because I had mentioned players at United Nations Relief Works Agency (for Palestinian Refugees in the Near East), UNRWA, I was advised to squelch it because there had been threats made against the lives of those UNRWA workers and highlighting their work could exacerbate the threat. It is complex and I was in way over my head. There were far too many dots for me to conne[illegible] into a cogent pattern.

Boots on the Ground

Environmentalists love to tell us we cannot just do one thing. I was changing on the inside but had no words. My world view *was* cracking; stones were moving. Imagine the stress on a structure when one stone moves. Jesus talked about the rejected stone becoming the cornerstone. The Palestinian women were changing me. Their lives were dedicated to loving ---their children who chafed under the boot of the occupation, their men who resisted and spent their lives in captivity. They endured the fear of death, inability to find a job and living with the resulting poverty, and constant oppression. They feared that their centuries-old home could be reduced to rubble if an Israeli official pulled a demolition order out of a drawer. It would become fifteen minutes work for an Israeli bulldozer built in the United States. The oppressors who circumscribed their existence and possibilities could tighten the thumbscrews at will. That was my "Holy Land" experience. But what could I do with it?

I had no neat presentation, no roadmap through the morass, no way to articulate what I was feeling. The images haunted me. The residue of my trip: shards, and shrapnel that I would have to forge into words to share the breadth and depth of that experience. Connect the dots.

Herstory

I am reading an African American theologian and scholar, Dr. Diana L. Hayes' description of the "wounding" of the African American community and their faithful courage which has brought forth so many sacred gifts in the United States. She writes:

> African American spirituality was forged in the fiery furnace of slavery in the United States. The ore was African in origin, in worldview, in culture, and in traditions. The coals were laid in the bowels of ships named, ironically, after Jesus and Christian virtues, which carried untold Africans to the Americas. The fire was stoked on the "seasoning islands" of the Caribbean or the "breeding"

plantations of the South where men, women and children of Africa were systematically and efficiently reduced to beasts of burden and items of private property. Yet those who came through those fires were not what they seemed. Despite the ungodly and oppressive forces applied against them, they forged a spirituality that encouraged hope and sustained faith, which enabled them to build communities to love and to model trust and to persevere in the persistent efforts to be free men and women they had been created to be…"[75]

Dr. Hayes described what my Palestinian trip had showed me. There is a commonality of suffering across cultures. On my second trip in January 2020 to Israel I walked beside the art of the Wall of Separation on the Palestinian side in Bethlehem, near the Banksy Hotel. Those images of the suffering and hope painted on that wall gave voice in this land no bigger than the state of New Jersey. The Wall of Separation art pricked the thick husk of the seed to let a little light in to germinate the fragile, tender hope of justice encapsulated within. Art and beauty have the embryos of new life. Saul Bellow said, "Unexpected intrusions of beauty. This is what life is."[76]

The African American experience of slavery and its kindred forms of brutal repression reverberate in the occupied Palestinian lands. Add a lockdown in a pandemic. Cry justice. Connect the dots but fear holds me back. Others are more conversant, they speak eloquently. Yet the only way I will ever know if my words are credible is to muster courage, acknowledge my weakness, and fear, is to tell my story. Stepping over my fears will require new ways of acting, a grown-up set of behaviors and walking in faith even when I cannot see my feet on the path.

---

[75] Diana L. Hayes, *Forged in a Fiery Furnace: African American Spiritu* (Maryknoll, NY: Orbis Books, 2012) 2, 3, 5.

[76] Saul Bellow, *Herzog,* (NY: Penguin Books, 1975) 237.

Embracing Change

There are several theological dots that are important in my life. Having been both a librarian and a pastor I want people to know from the get-go that their life and their story are part of God's story. And like God's story, it is sacred. I want them to see those connections. The meaning of those stories grew as I dealt with couples and mothers (I never had a father request baptism for his child, but times are changing), and grandmothers who wanted sacrament done in the prescribed method of their family. In the baptismal interview the parents and I begin to unpack the meaning of that sacrament and implications for the child's life. Frequently baptism's rich meaning would override the mechanics of a ceremony they had come to discuss. They stood in awe before God's promise to their beloved child. An ancient rite for the forgiveness of sins that preceded Jesus' dip in the Jordan was then infused with God's most Holy Spirit blessing and sustaining their child forever.

The Apostle Paul elucidates God creating for community as he claims the baptized, buried with Jesus Christ so that they may rise with him emerging from the waters now to be dressed in the clothes of faith. "They are neither Jew or Greek, slave or free, male or female, for all are one in Christ Jesus. If you belong to Christ, then you are Abraham's seed, and heirs according to the promise" (Gal 3:28-29 NIV). What a community, what a family, what a promise! It was a boatload for parents and me to ponder for those baptismal waters of the Creator, Christ and Holy Spirit bestow a whole new world! John announced those who thwarted God's reign would be on a collision course with God's life-giving purpose that those baptismal waters bestow. Jesus' baptism was not an insurance policy for lifelong happiness and mountaintop experiences! In Luke's telling Jesus' clothes were yet not dry from the Jordan waters before he is whisked into temptation. Luke ties baptism and wilderness testing together as part of the Christian life.

In Matthew's gospel we see up close and personal the demons, principalities nd powers that are squaring off against Jesus. This is an important battle him. It is ours too. One of the struggles of our life today is the porosity e notion of sin; it is most frequently viewed as a personal failure to stand squarely against the devil. Yet Jesus' temptation in the wilderness was much wider and its meanings may help clarify a notion that individuals, the church and culture are wrestling with today. Connect the dots.

Jesus' first temptation was a response to a basic human need; he had been in the desert for forty days and he was hungry. Instead of running to the bread aisle Jesus reminds the us that possessions and the controlling of possessions can trip up the divine-human balance. "Man does not live by bread alone" is the first tip-off that the bestowing the holy spirit will always force a conversation about what belongs to Caesar and what belongs to God. Filling our stomachs, bank accounts, corporations and even nation first must be in dialog with "the least of these." How choices are made is a much larger arena than "me, my, mine." Possessions are slippery slopes frequently disguised as cultural virtues and signs of God's favor. Note: those outside the bread aisle may not have those options.

Next the wily devil takes Jesus to the pinnacle, (who doesn't want to be there?), tells him to throw himself off and God will guard him, "lest he dash his foot against a stone." We live in a culture where "too big to fail" is bandied about in corporate parlance. Ever resourceful, the devil quotes scripture to Jesus but Jesus doesn't fall for the out-of-context proof texting gimmick. Jesus reminds the devil not to put God to the test. The temptation of unbridled power, ostentatious and showy, is idolatrous for it sees itself as demanding full allegiance, too big to be criticized, and rolling over resistance with crushing force.

Matthew's description of the third temptation resonates with those who feel something is missing after their own definitions of success have been met and they are still casting about for "something more." What good is all they have if no one reveres their accomplishments and power? Without acknowledgement no one can imagine the heights they have climbed, the shaping of the environment by their sheer force and grit. Veneration is needed, for the system bends to power, adulates possessions, and prostrates itself before the one who dominates. Besides others cannot see the view from the top. Prestige is needed to control the field of consciousness, th very air, so that the disguise of total control can be complete. Howe missing is the wide-angle lens which looks life across the spectrum of options and sees a field where discernment, deeper understanding, and compassion are possible. Hence the devil offers a one-dimensional notion of reality, and prestige fills the breathless stage. Connect the dots.

Sitting on That Dialogical Log

In my mind's eye I can envision the apostle Paul and Jesus sitting on that venerable Socratic log. The best in rhetoric and thought of the ancient Greek philosophers is replaced by two who set the Roman Empire abuzz in the first century. While talking about love Paul and Jesus are moving their discussion to a fuller context. Jesus focused his attention on institutions whose heartfelt impulses were to create good and ennoble the community. Yet he noted as their façades became institutionalized they concealed those very temptations of his desert days: possessions, prestige, and power. He chastised, subverted, and showed the baseness that is required to promote human enterprises that seek to become a container for their own non-negotiable definition of the "good."

Paul had a different take on the problem. He was transformed by the goodness of the message of the cross and realized that experience could crash and burn unless that message was able to convert hearts to that realm that Jesus repeatedly said was at hand. That message took nurture.

Jesus' experience in the wilderness had taught him that power, possessions, and prestige created a dualism of right/wrong, in/out, for us/opposing us that denies God's creation and purposes. Bathed in good ratings, intentionally or unintentionally, the institutions grew as did their shadows. Those who spoke from the cave of the heart on the edge of the community became pariahs and threats to institutional stability and growth that had been so carefully constructed. So there sits Jesus, "where two or three are gathered," and "All authority in heaven and earth has been given to me. Go therefore and make disciples of all nations, baptizing them in the name of the Father and Son and Holy Spirit and teaching them to obey everything that I have commanded you. And remember I am with you always, to the end of the age" (Mt 28: 19-20 NRSV). Lot of miles between those two utterances.

Paul focused on the post-resurrection Jesus. His conversion experience overcame blindness and his myopic attention on the rituals and forms of faithfulness and refocused on building a flourishing community of "fellow travelers to the grave," as Charles Dickens noted. It was in that mode of service, prayer, and gratefulness that Paul felt an energy and joy that propelled him into the center of church squabbles, chastising the slackers, lifting up service, thinking outside the box, traipsing all over the Eastern Mediterranean world, and cheerleading so the community could enjoy abundant life. He even stared down the gentiles, the Roman authorities and the temple leaders whose hearts were set on getting their own way. Perhaps, on closer examination, Jesus and Paul are sitting on a non-dialectic bench where both/and mindset is embedded in a relationship between the God who creates for community and those who know their great need of being a part of something bigger than themselves. Connect the dots.

In 313 Constantine…

Every confirmand connects that date with that emperor, for it is when Christianity started down the road to becoming the official religion of the Roman Empire, something like becoming the official sponsor for the Olympics. There would be lots of benefits. Roman emperors needed to be inordinately aware of what was going on around them and super-sensitive to undercurrents, and constantly looking over their shoulders, and sending ears to check activity at ground level. By 300 CE ten percent of the Roman Empire was Christian. They would not serve in the army; they believed serving in the legion was murder on a grand scale. This ran headlong into Roman ethics that believed that military valor was the greatest virtue. Christians could often serve as local enforcers, much like police officers. But in 303 CE Emperor Diocletian completed the Great Persecution where he destroyed churches, seized their property, removed Christians from any positions in the government, burned texts, and imprisoned priests and sent many to their deaths.

When it was Constantine's turn to be Emperor in 312 CE, he saw that it was the church that held the people together in strong bonds, He wisely surmised that the structure would be a good way to secure his reign. Whether Constantine had a vision of the Chi Rho symbol in the sky before he defeated a much larger army on the Milvian Bridge is debated, or whether his mother instilled Christianity in her son or whether she was introduced to it by her son. But in 313 the edict of Milan stopped the persecution of Christians and others who did not worship the Roman gods. It returned confiscated church property and established Sun Day, a day of rest. Whether it was to honor the Roman sun god, or the Son of God, is debated, it was nevertheless a day of rest, except for agricultural workers.

Constantine took Christians off the menu for lions in amphitheaters and banned publicly displayed gladiatorial games in 325 CE. Christians could be governmental officials and Constantine supported new basilicas, exempted certain taxes for clergy, and endowed the church with land. Between 324 and 330 CE he built a new Rome on the Bosporus which would be named Constantinople after himself. He "starved" temples to other gods by withdrawing his support of them. His court was filled with respected men from leading Roman families, even those who refused to convert, yet powerful positions went to the Christians. He was able to keep the tension between Christians and non-Christians in balance.

It wasn't until 380 CE, long after Constantine had died in 327 CE, that the Treaty of Thessalonica made Christianity the "official religion of the Holy Roman Empire." But the precedents of Constantine's conversion and reign are front and center in today's debates of the separation of church and state, the church as recipient of tax money, the use of force "to enforce peace," and the imposition of a moral code of the church as public policy. The intertwining of the empire and the church created many oxymorons in this new notion of church and state. The desert fathers and mothers took off, preferring the way of solitude to the path of "official sponsor" status conferred on the church. Those marginalized and persecuted ask,

"By whose authority?" The liberation theologians give voice to theology of the oppressed. Connect the dots.

Rummage Sales

It was the Rt. Rev. Mark Dyer who observed every five hundred years or so the church holds a rummage sale. Church sociologist Phyllis Tickle fleshed out what happened that necessitated those rummage sales.[77] She described the church as a cable of meaning that connects humanity to some power or purpose greater than itself. When the cable is strong humanity is secured by that cable of meaning. Within the cable are three strands, spiritual, corporeal and moral. They secure human life in meaningfulness, which is the function of religion. As long as nothing threatens the story cable, the three interconnecting strands function smoothly, religion is doing its job, answering the existential religious question, "Isn't there more?" But when one of the strands within the story cable is pockmarked or dinged, trouble is brewing.

For the last half century, the "spiritual but not religious" dialog has raged. The fallout of that discussion means that much of the church has become suspect. Questions about science, human sexuality, the universe and physics push against the Enlightenment's answers. What should the role of the church be as a property owner, as disseminator of the sacred story, as caregiver and educator, as a community of faith? Who is the faithful person? The church is being challenged and called out for its abuses and perversions as the story cable that holds meaning is being attacked, and new questions and insights are popping up like suckers on the trunk of a tree. Who exactly are we, what is our sacred story and how do we connect the dots now? [78]

The story cable works until a pockmark ruptures on the outside and chances are good that one or more of the three strands has been frayed as well. Sensing that threatened strand inside, it is opened and each strand

---

[77] Phyllis Tickle, *The Great Emergence* (Grand Rapids: Baker Books, 2008) 16.

[78] ibid., 34-38.

checked thoroughly before it is stuffed back in the story cable to be tightly wound with duct tape right at the place it has broken before. The church finds itself with things no longer needed. About every 500 years a rummage sale. Their themes have been :

> First Century Jesus and the beginning of the Church,
> Sixth Century Gregory the Great and the rise of Monasteries,
> Eleventh Century Schism of the Eastern and Western Churches,
> Sixteenth Century Protestant Reformation,
> Twentieth-first Century Decline of Enlightenment, Christendom and the Digital Age.[79]

Tickle looked at the 500-year cycle and described what had happened when the cable of consensual illusion, the common imagination was damaged. For example, John Wycliffe troubled the waters with his insistence that the scriptures be read in the language of the people in the 1300s. Enter Martin Luther, *sola scriptura, scriptura sola* Luther, with his emphasis on the written text. Armed with hammer and nails he headed to the door of the Wittenberg Church on October 31, 1417 and nailed his 95 DYI projects on the door.

With the advent of the printing press in 1440 the printed word was readily accessible, and literacy would skyrocket. The church was no longer the absolute authority, people could read and question for themselves. There was much to question. For instance, the church had two popes: a Roman pope, Urban VI and a French pope, Clement VII in Avignon, France. Both claimed to be the successor to Peter.

The explosion of information fostered new questions. Rationalism and science burst on the scene. From science, to literature, to government there was a new day. Serfs were no longer agricultural commodities, they

ibid., For Pope Gregory and the rise of monasticism, 25-26; for the Reformation, 46; for the split of Orthodoxy from the Roman Empire, see Phyllis Tickle, *rence Christianity* (Grand Rapids: Baker Books, 2012) 172-176.

moved to the cities. There was a merchant economy, no longer was land its currency. Gunpowder revolutionized warfare in the newly emerging city states. Greed grew right beside new methods and markets.

Arab-Christian tensions were fomented by the church's exploration, crusades, and warfare. The Ottoman armies captured Constantinople in 1453, forcing the intellectual community of Orthodoxy to emigrate to Europe. They brought with them their vast literature of the ancient world, mathematics and science, ancient languages, and the ability to interpret the wisdom of that world. Music of the renaissance flourished in the local idiom, no longer hidebound by classical forms. Learned men like Machiavelli questioned forms of government. The cable of consensual illusion was besieged. Chaos reigned and war broke out, with costly results for Europe. But when the dust settled, Protestantism was firmly embedded in northern Europe and the rupture proved good for the Catholic Church as well. Challenged by the list of abuses in the church, they cleaned up their act and the Roman Catholic church grew. That is a benefit, although a painful one; the rupture of the cable of consensual illusion, both parties can grow. Rummage sales are good for both parties have cleaning up to do.

Sale Today

There has been a foundational concern raised by the inquiries of Freud and Jung on what it means to be human, and Einstein introduced the quantum world, the world of unseen things floating around in a cosmos where we could now destroy human life on this planet. Heisenberg's Uncertainty Principle said you can measure the speed of a particle or you can measure its location but you cannot measure both simultaneously, for the more you know of the speed the less you know of its location and vice versa. Can you see absolute truth crashing into the wall of observation wherein the act of observing changes the thing observed? Liberation theologians noted theology from the underside. Truth has been demoted; its capital T gone. A little physics shook the church and now a bevy of questions swirled in the religious realm. Albert Schweitzer posed the question w Jesus of Nazareth the same as Jesus of Western thought and scholarsh

It opened floodgates of religious scholarship and conservatism as well as freedom to look outside the compound for alternative ways of being, and cross fertilizations of religions worldwide. Changing understandings of role of family and sexual orientation has hammered the cable of meaning and authority. The repercussions of the broken cable of meaning reach down many church aisles and into the public square.

This is my backstory, struggling to put my experience of Palestine into the cable of meaning and hoping that might be meaningful to someone else. My cable has been hammered. As an older person in this maelstrom, I wonder if previous church rummage sales have been as disquieting as this one. Time is accelerated. The James Russell Lowell hymn notes, "New occasions teach new duties/Time makes ancient good uncouth/ They must upward still, and onward/Who would keep abreast of truth." But as I start to determine just exactly where I am standing Phyllis Tickle comes charging in and says, "Oh, and another thing!"

Spiritual but Not Religious

The Split between the Eastern and Western Churches in the eleventh century was over *filioque,* literally translated "from the son."The scope of the debate was spread over Europe, the Middle East, and North Africa. Like the Reformation after it, there were economic, political, and cultural questions swirling in the air. But where the rubber met the road was the question, from where does the Holy Spirit come.

"From God alone," shouted the Eastern Church Patriarch of Constantinople Michael Cerularius, as he anathematized Pope Leo IX, (who ironically had died before his delegation had reached Constantinople) thus strengthening the claim of the incarnational church of incense and icons.[80] The Orthodox Church engaged the body, soul, and heart fully in worship. Why? Because the Orthodox Church finds God sensorily, in rich fabrics, candles everywhere, painted icons, and chanting to evoke the Divine, the whole

---

yllis Tickle, *The Age of the Spirit* (Grand Rapids: Baker Books, 2014) 102.

of us engaged with the whole of God. The Orthodox Church experiences God communally, through the Trinity: God, Christ and Holy Spirit.

The Roman Church excommunicated the Orthodox Church, insisting the Holy Spirit preceded from God *and* Jesus Christ. The Roman Catholic Church "went north." The cliché refers not to going north into Europe, but north to the head, a logical and rational form of worship, a cerebral God. The theological underpinnings were because the Holy Spirit proceeded from both God and Christ, *filioque,* the Holy Spirit did not quite have the standing of the two senior partners in the Godhead. Form, discipline, and structure shaped the Roman experience. The church could gauge its pleasing God by the successes that characterized its life, and the structure itself as indicative of God's favor.

Truly the Holy Spirit was left to blow where it will, and while it wasn't corralled into the fold of intellectual assertion and structure, the rupture has never truly healed. In the Trinity there is balance, a divine dance, a wondrous community of otherness and intimacy, an inflowing of friendship which is heard in Jesus' words, "I call you friends," which answers our existential question of "Is there more?" [81] The focus is on community, freely giving and freely receiving between the partners as they work and weave life together. More community, less competition. Today, "spiritual not religious" is speaking through Emergence Christianity, calling for a communal ecclesiology. Fearing a too precise and defined God in the box, those churches welcome the mystery of the divine encounter. Connect the dots now. A thousand-year-old pock in the cable of meaning has split wide open and it affects Christianity and religions worldwide. While being examined it asks how then shall we live? The emerging answer is that Holy Spirit is a key and fully empowered player! The dots that looked like buckshot on the side of a barn are beginning to have an emerging pattern. I may have to use my imagination and squint a lot.

---

[81] Richard Rohr with Jon Sweeney, *The Divine Dance* (New Kensington, PA: Whitaker House, 2016*) 159.*

Elaine Eachus

Dancing Toward Meaning

I am both embarrassed and hopeful in saying that I am moving downstream. I have a fair number of dents and dings in my ancient craft, the result of many storms, yet I am moving with the current. I am noticing repetitions and patterns in those dots that may suggest new horizons ahead. Some of the dots seem to becoming parts of new settings and old assumptions revisited.

This pandemic has created "time out," away from unregulated human contact to be present here in this very spot. My husband and I have noticed with a fierce pleasure and amazement the things that are literally happening under our noses. We both photograph the natural world that we have seen within 1,000 feet of our home. He will come home from a walk with half dozen new photographs on his phone. We think about putting up the hummingbird feeder although our patio partners did not show up last winter.

Frustratingly I have a deeper appreciation of bringing the harvest to the table as I have cooked unceasingly, since the COVID-19 inception. I think about food a lot. What flavors and tastes will complement the other flavors at the meal? I even think about the building of layers of flavor in each dish with herbs growing outside my kitchen door and spices from the warmer countries. I have experimented and found many Mediterranean and less-than-familiar cuisines healthy and pleasurable, as in the vegan cuisine my granddaughters have embraced.

Another expression of this novel experience is noticing the relentless diminishment that is part of the harvest of age. It is OK. It is not resignation, nor guilt that accompanies disappointment or failure. It is the other side of having had the experience: appreciation for what has been given, for what has been learned, for seeing other players in their humanness, their vulnerability, woundedness, and yes, their glory. There is no subtraction, nothing is written out of the script. What is written is the awareness that how we respond does make a difference.

Hendricks Chapel at Syracuse University is modeled after Monticello. Inside the dome are written God's operating instructions in gold letters: "Ye shall know the truth, and the truth shall set you free. Not that we have lordship over your faith but are helpers of your joy. God is a spirit, and they that worship Him must worship Him in spirit and in truth." I was seventeen and a freshman when I first saw those words. Van Gogh, near the end of his life as he was painting all those wheat fields at Arles, noted that he was beginning to "get yellow." I am staring at all those dots and it feels like I am starting to "get it" too. Some things take a long time.

Many things have been dragged out for church's rummage sale. Grandiose schemes and power wielded for power's sake, self-aggrandizement, screens where the shadow hides, scabs over old wounds, assumptions of knowing the Truth, perfectionistic stances and moralistic postures which serve as a barrier to keep joy and surprise out. Denial of vulnerability, weakness, and decrepit forms of worship, rugged individualism, (which is loneliness in thick clothing), are in the pile. Getting rid of these will give more room for what is up ahead. Just thinking about living without all that weight feels lighter. I suspect there might be dancing, reunions, beauty rediscovered, shared, and appreciated, as the dots are now seen as converging in new configurations in a community where the spirit blows where it will. Our task is to look carefully at the cable of meaning, check the strands and feel the refreshing winds blowing all over the world to put together meaning and purpose while we walk into the future of an amazing, mysterious and fragile world.

GRACEFUL

Floating, a slight twitch, and the yellow maple effortlessly glided
against an uncharacteristic azure November day unremarkable
amid the bazillion soft sentinels guarding our yard.
It fell gracefully.

Not caught in the torrents of autumnal winds that pluck dead
branches easily as a child picking dandelions no ecstatic
whirls of dervishes in gusty dance never
wrested from her mother's arms like a Palestinian child in Nakba
nor scrunched homeless on an underpass bed.
It fell gracefully.

Grace comes from an unshakable trust in the currents
knowing each has a context and,
at last a confident letting go uncertain if descent will be
rough sea'd or smooth sailing.

Graceful in the interplay of I and thou, assured thus
one bright fragile joy fulfilled its destiny.
Most do it, most graceful. Most blessed. Most welcomed.
Purpose (It gave me breath). Path. Peace.

THE NORTHERN GARDENER

Random Gardens

Random gardens are tricky. They are sometimes hard to spot. When discovered they seem out of place, and we are jolted by our discovery. A young adult book whose title I have long forgotten tells of a young woman who was incarcerated and used her time in the exercise yard to discover the many kinds of flowers that grew there. She was amazed at the sheer number when she took to time to look at what she had taken for granted as she walked the perimeter. Their miniature beauty and intricacy delighted her.

We recently went to Mexico, Grand Cayman, Jamaica and the Dominican Republic as day stops on a cruise. Some areas had rocky soil, hilly terrain and difficult, crowded conditions, some starkly barren. It was not the palatial settings we see in those slick magazines of Florida living. My first thought was to look at those places with my first-world mindset and imagine what could be done to make them better. I had to restrain my impulse to manage and rearrange things like a bougainvillea blooming in an old five-gallon paint can. I saw the graceful curve of a majestic old tree offering its gift of shade over tiny houses where children were playing. I saw tiny flowers growing in the sandy transitions of coastline.

In Jamaica we went to a river waterhole high up in the hills where vines competed with trees for the sunshine. Children and adults screamed with delight and terror as they jumped, swung or slipped into the rushing river. That random garden was a complete picture, as I imagine the Master Gardener intended, with folks enjoying and laughing.

One Sunday after church I saw an extremely creative parishioner, photograph a tall pine tree in the south yard. Armed with his iPad camera he marched to within striking distance of the trunk, aimed his weapon upward and shot. He showed me a thoughtful picture he had taken of the tree with the predominant feature being the trunk with its rough chunky bark. Atop his image, seemingly far in the distance, were the branches and needles of the manufacturing facility that exchanged carbon dioxide and oxygen, and the noisy habitat of squawking green parrots in the churchyard.

His act reminded me of what is needed for random gardens to flourish. They require notice and appreciation. The flowers in the prison yard, the river garden in Jamaica, the solitary pine where parrots congregate, all need our eye to appreciate the beauty which surrounds us. Taking the time to notice and bringing our unique perspective to a random garden we become co-creators with God. We can see and enjoy this beautiful world with fresh eyes. We discover places and spaces as God intends, a beauty that is part and parcel of existence. It stretches our capacity to appreciate the gift of life.

THE INCREDIBLE MYSTERY OF JOY: HOW THE DIVINE TRANSFORMS OUR DOUBTS AND FEARS

Texts: Exodus 34:29-35, Luke 9:28-43a

When our first son was born at an Army post in Alabama, Alan, my husband, and I were exuberant parents. This was back when fathers were not allowed in delivery rooms. Andy made his debut at about 10 p.m. on a Tuesday night. There were a couple of things that highlighted Andy's birth. The first was when the doctor went to tell my husband our child was here, my husband's first question was if he were a father of a boy or a girl. "Your wife wants to tell you," the doctor said.

"Well, can I see the baby?" ACE inquired.

"Oh no," Dr. Shulman said. "He hasn't been circumcised." That kind of blew my announcement!

The second thing happened later that night when I awoke and rang for the nurse. "What time is it?"

"It's after twelve," the nurse replied.

I was still confused. "Is that noon or midnight?" I queried.

"It's a little after midnight," she continued.

"Oh, I couldn't tell because of the light behind the bed."

"There is no light behind your bed," she said.

"Oh, you can't see it?" She shook her head. I fell silent. I could. There was a light that flooded the room that emanated from behind the bed. What could it be? My father had died nine months before Andy was born. Maybe it was my father's presence. Time went on and I had all but forgotten about it. Maybe it was the epidural that had been administered. I don't recall mentioning it to anyone for years, but I can still feel the intensity and whiteness of that light.

Transfiguration Sunday is the time after all the wonders of Jesus' coming into our world, we still haven't gotten the total picture yet. There is more to God's incredible gift to us, mysterious with its implications extending far beyond the moment. Jesus, Luke tells us, is the Son of God, the Messiah. God reveals Jesus' intimate relationship with Moses, the lawgiver, and Elijah, the prophet on a mountaintop where we along with Peter, James and John can see, but perhaps not comprehend.

In November 2018 voters in the state of Florida passed Amendment 4 to the Florida Constitution which gave voters in the state of hanging chads and counties that can't count votes the largest single expansion of the right to vote in America since the 26th Amendment gave 18-year-olds enfranchisement. Passing Amendment 4 promoted full citizenship and permits more people to participate in the electoral process, thus ending a blatant Jim Crow policy and encouraging reintegration of convicted felons.

Great! What does this have to do with Jesus' experiences in a cloud with Moses and Elijah up on a mountain twenty centuries ago? That Florida amendment gave 1.4 million citizens who have been living and working in our communities the right to vote in Florida. That's huge! Transfiguration is about seeing a whole new context that changes perspectives forever. Regrettably the 2021 Florida legislature has introduced bills that would chip away at the intent of Amendment 4 creating more obstacles to voting for those rehabilitated felons.

Disenfranchisement of convicted of felonies is widespread. Yet we know each of us is capable of doing wrong. Our scriptures tell us Moses killed an Egyptian, David had Bathsheba's husband killed, Peter denied being Jesus' follower and Paul had persecuted Christians before his Damascus road experience. Yet murderer, adulterer and contract killer, denier of Jesus and persecutor, all repented and went on to serve God. Seeing things in a different context changes everything, and great good and restoration can come from that.

God's justice, his righteousness, is about restorative justice. Luke's story of the prodigal son who "sinned against heaven" was welcomed and graciously restored into his father's house with a joyous feast. Jesus told the adulterous woman she was no longer accused; now go and live faithfully in her community. Where we get hung up is that wrongdoing affects more than just the immediate victim and the perpetrator. We live in communities and we are interconnected. This extended effect and interconnectedness requires us to consider the ancillary effect of a punishment on the community. Voting is an act of community caring. Parents who vote influence their children's attitudes about voting and participation in voting. Restoring justice increases the joy and restores a lost sheep to the fold, and a neighbor to our community.

Dr. Martin Luther King Jr. said that we are commanded to love our enemies, but we didn't have to like them. I take that to mean that we are to make sure everyone gets to participate in God's restorative justice, where there are no second-class citizens. Perhaps that is why there are over 2,000 verses in the Bible about caring for those who are on the fringes, the poor, the alien, the widow, and the stranger. We are all welcomed at God's table of abundance where each is loved. There we see how God created in goodness and wants us to build on it. There, loving our enemy is enough, even when the enemy opposes us.

One of the shortest books in the Bible is the letter from the Apostle Paul to Philemon. It's a classic. It's about transforming life into unimagined new life for a slave and his community! Paul, in jail, is writing to his good friend. Philemon is obviously a good guy who has done much good and wants to continue. Paul thanks God for all the hospitality Philemon displays in the house church he hosts.

Paul has a tiny favor to ask. In language drenched with irony Paul asks, but doesn't command. Would Philemon would welcome back his runaway slave, Onesimus, who had wound up in the same prison as Paul? Welcome him home, Philemon, not as a slave, but as a brother!

We can almost see Philemon spit out his morning coffee as he reads the letter. *Bring him back not as a slave but as a brother in our faith? Let's hope none of my other slaves gets wind of this! This could be my ruin!* Paul says to welcome your slave as if he were Paul coming to visit. And Paul will repay any costs or damages, just put it on his account. *Yeah right, from his prison account?* Then in the final delicious twist Paul says he knows Philemon will grant this favor and will probably do it with more ruffles and flourishes than Paul could imagine. After all Paul and Philemon are brothers in Christ and that changes everything. I can imagine Philemon hiding the letter lest anyone else read it. If Paul is right and Philemon did welcome a slave as a brother in Christ, it could change everything. Fears and doubts on one hand, a changed social order and incredible mystery on the other. And it is obvious that Philemon is convinced by Paul's argument for this letter is part of the canon of faith. Philemon was changed, transformed, and a slave was set free!

The ancient Israelites are dealing with an incredible mystery and they know the consequences. We heard in our text when Moses comes down from Mt. Sinai after his tête-à-têtes with God his face is luminous and shining like the sun. The Israelites are no dummies. They know no one has ever looked on the face of God and survived. Yet here comes Moses shiny-faced and bursting with God's plans for harmonious living in covenant with God. Maybe Moses has had life-changing experiences on that mountain, but the Israelites don't want to get burned. *"We'll listen to what God said but cover your face, Moses."*

Counselors and chaperones for teens who have gone off to camp, mission trips or work camp experiences have a session the last night where they gather those who have had life-changing experiences. That night the talk is about "going back home." It is a let-them-down-gently time for not everyone will have had the tremendous feeling of warmth, awe, and delight that the youth have experienced. Going home may feel like cold water in the face. The hometown folks may be right there with the Israelites who are viewing Moses with suspicion and fear. They are not ready to surrender their control and power for a long shot which they suspect could ultimately be more powerful and life changing than life as they now know it. The Apostle Paul realizes that in 2 Corinthians 3:7-18. He says the Israelites wanted Moses to wear the veil so folks will notice that and not become too enthralled as the laws of Moses are being read.

But, Paul asserts, there is an alternative. It is the realization that God is not a set of rules chiseled on stone. God creates for relationship, with us! It is wondrous, unexplainable through logic or reason which ironically, is the gold standard of the Enlightenment. It cannot be set down in a finite equation nor parsed out in finer and finer definitions of human behavior and the law. Paul says it is seeing that there is "nothing between us and God, our faces shining with the brightness of his face. And so we are transfigured much like the Messiah, our lives gradually becoming brighter and brighter and more beautiful as we become like him" (2 Cor 3:18 *MSG*).

Dr. King said that "love is the only force capable of transforming an enemy into a friend." So how do we get there? Where is that deep joy of the divine in our lives? The Latin root of the word religion is *religare,* means to bind together. The monumental task is to bring together some cohesive whole or narrative amid the unsolvable and unfathomable mystery of our experience. The other Latin word, *religere,* has a different nuance. It means to go over again. The Israelites found they could look at someone who had had a direct experience with God and live, and Peter, James and John found their faltering response to the mystery of the transfigured Jesus exceeded their limits and abilities. But taking these two foci of religious life, bind together and paying attention, we discover there are many epiphanies disclosing the presence of God in our lives. I am not alone in an experience I cannot fully explain. Regardless of religious affiliation, or lack of it, most Americans today report they have had an experience that does not fit into our rational cubby holes, but that inexplicable experience has shaped their perceptions and actions. Which is, as Thomas Merton said, we see it, but we are not skilled in describing it. Mysticism has been called as navel gazing, self-delusional and dreamily confused. It is frequently paired with the occult. Mysticism has been described as starting with mist, having "I" in the middle and ending with schism.

But today there are new ways to describe that part of our experience which we are not skilled in describing. The poet Mary Oliver wrote,

I don't know exactly what prayer is.

I do know how to pay attention…"[82]

She was a mystic of the natural world and probably the most quoted poet of contemporary preachers because of her way of encountering life which encourages a theological vision of the world with a deep love of neighbor and a relative lack of theological sophistication that challenges the cynicism of life today. Mary Oliver saw and wrote about the act of noticing and cherishing relationships the Creator perceives as beautiful. "What I write about neither begins nor ends with the human world."[83]

Her poem, "Coming to God: First Days" tells of learning to kneel into the world of the inscrutable:

Then I will move no more than the leaves of a tree

On a day of no wind

…like a wanderer who has come home at last."[84]

Thomas Merton had a mystical experience as he left the Abbey of Gethsemani on the way to the dentist. His transforming experience was

---

[82] Mary Oliver, "The Summer Day," *New and Selected Poems* (Boston: Beacon Press, 1992) 94.

[83] https://christiancentury.org/article/faith-matters/remembering-mary-oliver-and-her-prose January 24, 2019

[84] Mary Oliver, "Coming to God: First Days," *Thirst* (Boston: Beacon Press, 2006) 23.

being united to all those strangers on the corner of Walnut and Fourth Streets:

> This sense of liberation from illusory difference was such a relief and such a joy to me that I almost laughed out loud…I have the immense joy of being a man, member of a race in which God Himself became incarnate. As if the sorrows and stupidities of the human condition could overwhelm me, now I realize what we all are. And if only everybody could realize this! Far beyond the circumscribed borders of human experience this! But it cannot be explained. There is no way of telling people that they are all walking around shining like the sun.[85]

Thomas Merton, Mary Oliver, you and I and those who hunger and thirst for righteousness have to learn to use the tools of the poetic, the symbolic, metaphoric, and the music of the spheres to kneel into the world of the inscrutable. Here we learn reality transfigures us too. As we honor and delight in God, we understand God's delight in welcoming us and getting us to notice our earth home in all its mystery and wonder.

Mary Oliver challenges us to live transformed lives.

> "Tell me, what else should I have done?
> Doesn't everything die at last, and too soon?
> Tell me what is it you plan to do
> With your one wild and precious life?"[86]

Our one wild and precious life! Amen.

---

[85] Thomas Merton, *Conjectures of a Guilty Bystander* (NY: First Image Books edition, 1968) 154.

[86] "The Summer Day," 94.

STEEPLE BELLS

Bells still echo from the steeple as we wait for word, wine, bread
As our forebears brought the future, make our worship Spirit-led.
Grant us, Lord, that we may follow in your purpose, truth and grace
For tomorrow is our passion: all your people see your face.

Bells are chiming 'cross the valley; river flows, refreshing, pure
For this moment is God's cosmos brought so life will now endure.
Flourish and proclaim Christ's story, share the sacred, gospel plan.
Stand together, teaching justice, lift each child, woman, man.

May the steeple bells be ringing when we too, return to you
Others looking for a future, see their image cast anew
Born of sacrifice and wisdom, hearts committed west to east
Caring for the least and last one, seated first a mercy's seat.

Hymn Tune: Beach Spring 8.7.8.7.D

WALKING IN THE LIGHT

If I don't get to Bethl'hem for the breaking of the dawn
Will you tell those who're gathered that I am moving on?
I am walking in the light now, I have pierced the darkest night.
I am walking in the light now, holding fast to God's own hand.

If I didn't see you clearly, if I didn't love you dearly
Look up the light still shines, it can flood unyielding lines
For we're bathed in golden starlight, we are all God's saints in time.
For we're walking in the light now, holding fast to God's own hand.

In the city of mangers there are no strangers,
We walk by faith and not sight, life's mysteries made bright.
We are free of our obsessions, true joy is our possession
We are walking in the light now, holding fast to God's own hand.

So on with your journey, we'll meet in the dawn
For we are the witness that life will be reborn.
We'll look back at the past now, and we'll see God's grand design.
For we're soaring in the light now, wings that bring God's peace divine.

Hymn Tune: Natalie Sleeth, *In the Bulb There Is a Flower*

NORTHERN GARDENER

Welcome Home

When sod came for our church garden, we could literally put down roots. One couple in the church bought it and laid it. The grass makes the garden such a welcoming space! It delineates and unites. To celebrate we dedicated three memorial plaques. Now we can water the sod and the garden and watch our completed garden grow. Ahh! The garden symbolizes a place of rest and refreshment for our souls. It is a delight to walk to church beside the garden. It just feels good, like a welcome home.

The Israelites could taste the joy when they got back home after the Babylonian exile. How wonderful it would be to sleep in their own beds in their own homes and watch their crops and flocks grow. Ahh! But something happens when God restores us (or our garden). God does not bring us to the same place. We have had different experiences; we have been changed. Our context is different.

Isaiah 49 shares God's idea of the homecoming with the Israelites. It is not iced tea on the patio. God says welcome home, but I have plans for you. It's wonderful you are home. You have come through a difficult time. You have learned lessons and I have heard your cries. Now this is my vision for you.

"It is too light a thing that you should be my servant
to raise up the tribes of Jacob
and to restore the survivors of Israel;
I will give you as a light to the nations,

That my salvation may reach to the end of the earth." Isaiah 49:6 NRSV

With the coming of the sod, we completed a beautiful garden and a peaceful respite in God's presence. It will be wonderful to see how we will use it for light for the world and the salvation to reach to the ends of the earth.

EPILOGUE

Dance

Like birds we have been given wings
So we can soar across the stage.
Like tops we have been given a spin.
So we spin until we can't anymore.
In the midst of this soaring and flying
Turning and spinning,
We find a fire just beginning.
This is our true self.

Our granddaughter was 11 years old when she wrote her poem "Dance." A competitive dancer who also sings and plays the violin, this sixth grader was given the opportunity to write a poem celebrating dance as part of a unit on poetry in her school. Her poem was ultimately selected by Betty Bertaux as the text for her composition, "Dance" for the Fairfax Children's Chorus 2012 project, *The Poetry of Music: Shall We Dance?*

Printed in the United States
by Baker & Taylor Publisher Services